FANTASTIC
ORIGAMI
SEA CREATURES

20 INCREDIBLE PAPER MODELS

HISAO FUKUI

TUTTLE Publishing

Tokyo | Rutland, Vermont | Singapore

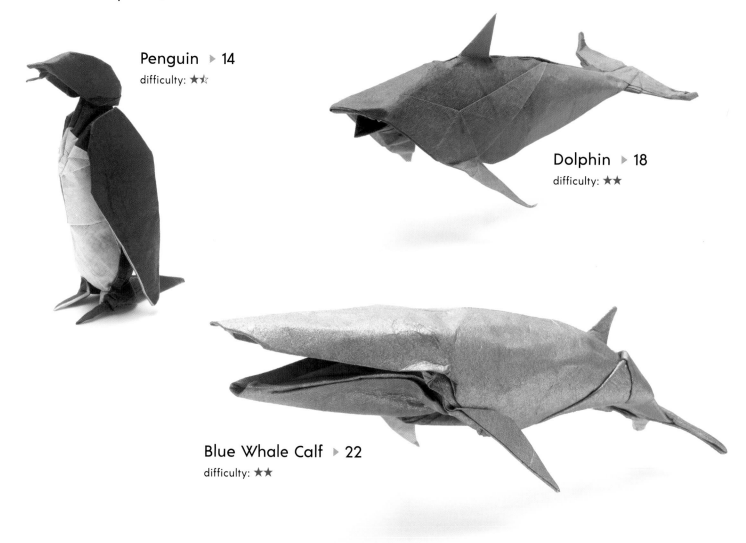

PART 2: SALTWATER FISH

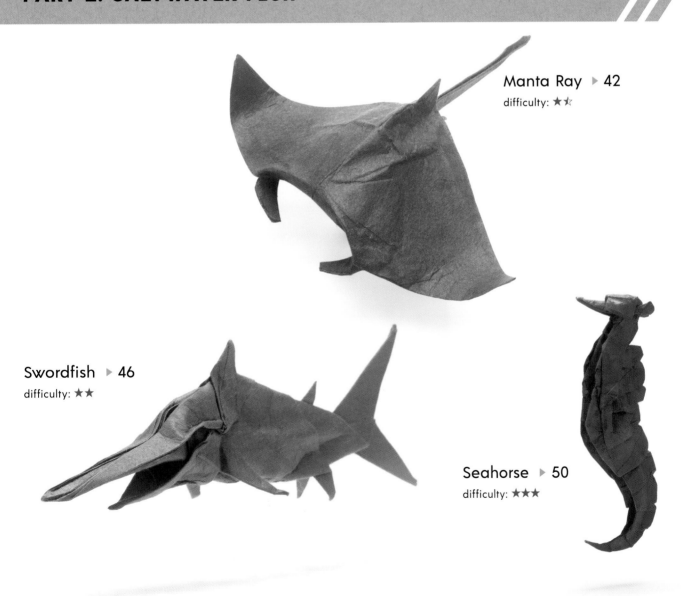

PART 3: FRESHWATER CREATURES

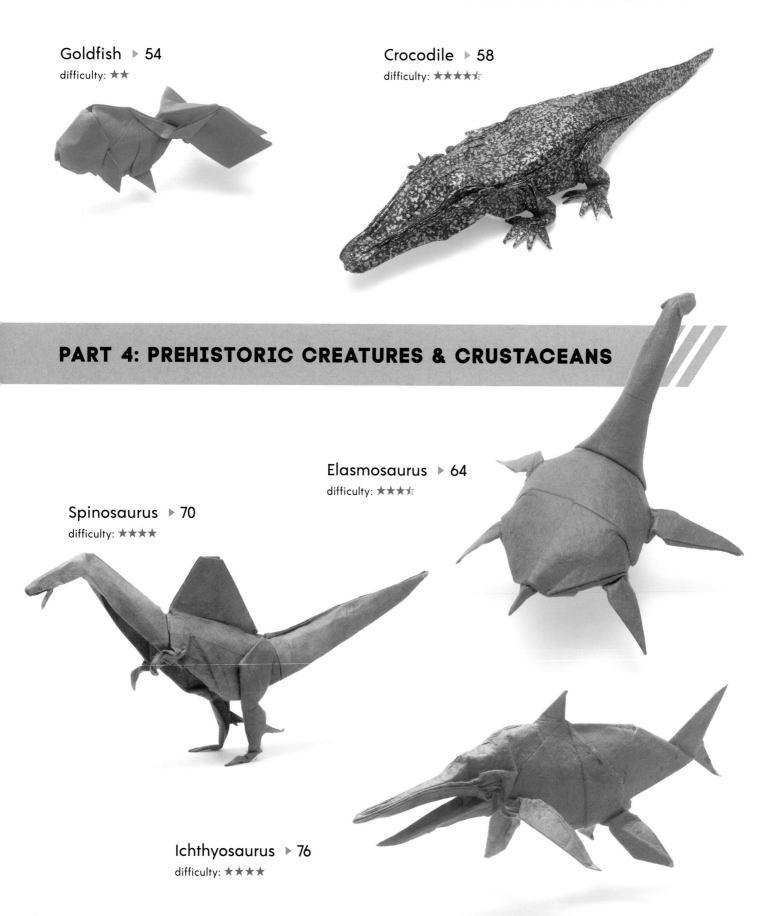

PART 4: PREHISTORIC CREATURES & CRUSTACEANS

PART 5: AQUATIC INVERTEBRATES

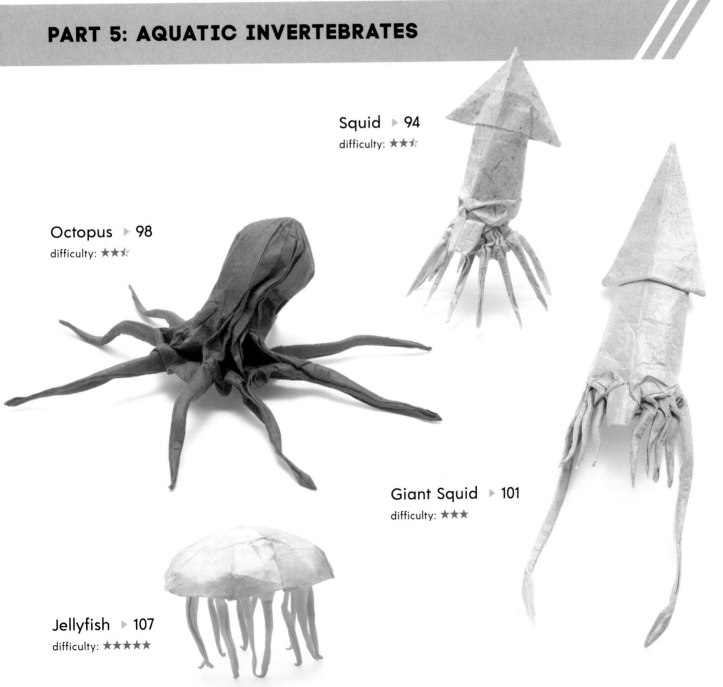

WHY I WROTE THIS BOOK

I decided to publish *Fantastic Origami Sea Creatures* in response to demand from readers who've enjoyed my other origami animal books. The strong positive reaction confirmed that interest in lifelike origami models is deep and wide, and I'm grateful for the support of all my readers!

This book presents a broad range of creatures that live in and around the water (saltwater and fresh), but I also have other books in Japanese that focus primarily on land animals, as well as a book on flying creatures (*Fantastic Origami Sea Creatures*), which was recently published in English by Tuttle Publishing.

Folding lifelike origami models is an art. The paper must be folded many times and in surprising ways to create a figure that closely resembles the look of animals, dinosaurs, insects, and so on.

Although folding these lifelike forms may seem daunting at first glance, each model begins with a stage called "basic folds,"* which simplifies the operation. After the basic folding is complete, I provide step-by-step instructions on how to produce more realistic and complex forms. The basic folds itself can be time-consuming, but it's usually not difficult—people of practically any age or skill level can accomplish it. After completing the basic folds stage, you don't necessarily need to follow the rest of the steps exactly as specified. You can change small details such as the shape of the wings, position of the head, etc. to taste to make your origami unique.

What sets lifelike origami apart from other simpler forms is that the finished products are three-dimensional and have many curved surfaces. You will often need to gently shape the model as a finishing touch to make the origami look just right. Sometimes, it may even take a few days to make small adjustments. Use the photos in this book as a reference for your adjustments. I recommend applying glue to your models so they hold their shape over long periods. See page 12 for details. I recommend the challenge of using glue to anyone who is beyond the beginner level. However, first-time folders are welcome to try it as well. I recommend practicing by folding the entire model at least one time before deciding to try one with glue applied—once the glue sets, there's no going back to fix earlier mistakes!

Generally speaking, Japanese paper (*washi*) will produce the best results for the models described in this book. It is pliable, natural-feeling, not prone to tearing, and it takes well to being moistened or glued. But in certain instances, commercially available origami paper (*kami*) is preferable—particularly for use when practicing. When using this sort of paper, I recommend using the thinnest paper you can find.

The models in this book range from relatively easy to quite challenging in terms of difficulty. To assist beginners, I've included detailed views for the more difficult procedures. If a given step seems confusing, look ahead to the next diagram for hints.

I hope you enjoy *Fantastic Origami Sea Creatures*!

—Hisao Fukui

> **Note**
>
> *Basic Folds: In this book, each model has a stage called "basic folds." In this stage, you should follow the instructions exactly. However, after this stage is complete, feel free to make minor adjustments, such as slightly adjusting folding angles and distances depending on your taste. The variations in the shape of the final product is part of the charm of lifelike origami.

A GUIDE TO THE FOLDING SYMBOLS

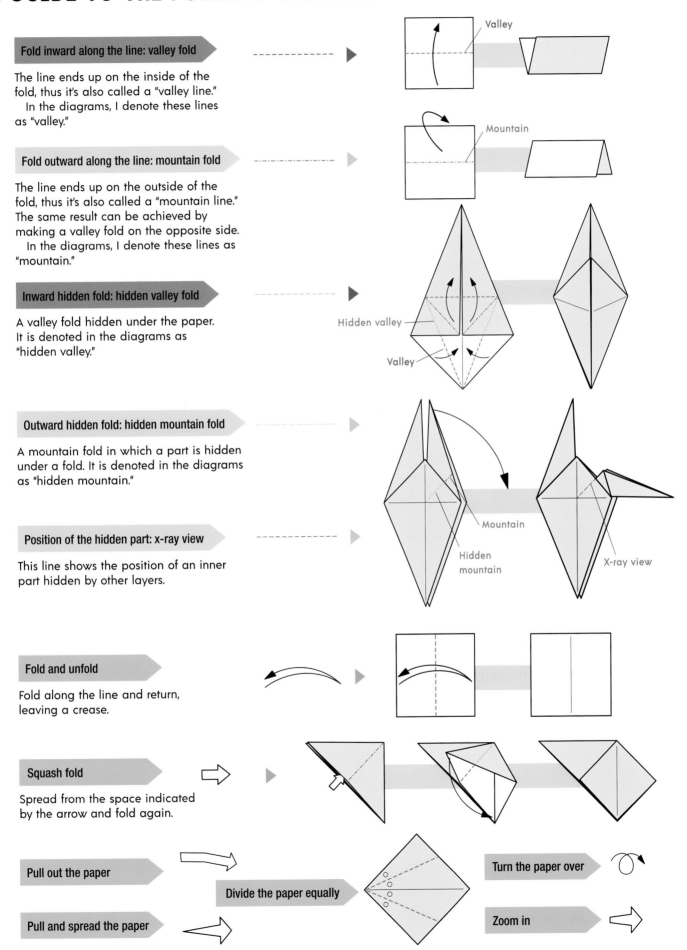

Fold inward along the line: valley fold

The line ends up on the inside of the fold, thus it's also called a "valley line."
In the diagrams, I denote these lines as "valley."

Valley

Fold outward along the line: mountain fold

The line ends up on the outside of the fold, thus it's also called a "mountain line." The same result can be achieved by making a valley fold on the opposite side.
In the diagrams, I denote these lines as "mountain."

Mountain

Inward hidden fold: hidden valley fold

A valley fold hidden under the paper. It is denoted in the diagrams as "hidden valley."

Hidden valley

Valley

Outward hidden fold: hidden mountain fold

A mountain fold in which a part is hidden under a fold. It is denoted in the diagrams as "hidden mountain."

Mountain

Hidden mountain

Position of the hidden part: x-ray view

This line shows the position of an inner part hidden by other layers.

X-ray view

Fold and unfold

Fold along the line and return, leaving a crease.

Squash fold

Spread from the space indicated by the arrow and fold again.

Pull out the paper

Divide the paper equally

Turn the paper over

Pull and spread the paper

Zoom in

SPECIALIZED FOLDING PROCEDURES

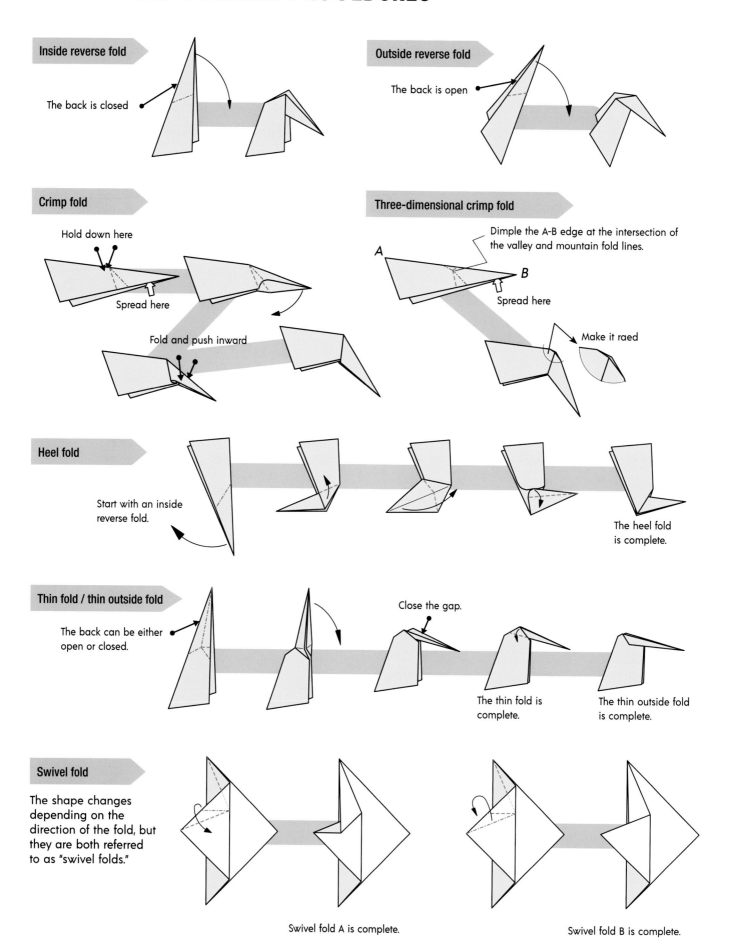

Inside reverse fold

The back is closed

Outside reverse fold

The back is open

Crimp fold

Hold down here

Spread here

Fold and push inward

Three-dimensional crimp fold

Dimple the A-B edge at the intersection of the valley and mountain fold lines.

A

B

Spread here

Make it raed

Heel fold

Start with an inside reverse fold.

The heel fold is complete.

Thin fold / thin outside fold

The back can be either open or closed.

Close the gap.

The thin fold is complete.

The thin outside fold is complete.

Swivel fold

The shape changes depending on the direction of the fold, but they are both referred to as "swivel folds."

Swivel fold A is complete.

Swivel fold B is complete.

Sink fold

Fold through step ④ of the Frog Base (page 10) for this example.

Crease the top point in half sharply and then open up the paper completely.

Re-form the folds at the center into mountain fold lines.

Refold the Frog Base folds while inverting the center section.

This completes the sink fold.

Rabbit ear

The rabbit ear fold is complete.

Pleat fold

Make a valley fold, and then bisect the flap with a mountain fold.

This completes the pleat fold.

Folding order

If the lines have a number next to them, follow the order and fold accordingly.

Wrap and re-form layers

Crease along the valley line.

Spread.

Spread again.

Open the flap.

Fold back into the previous shape, but keep the section between A and B flat.

In progress.

Bring the ABC triangle up and inward.

The layers are re-formed.

※ In this book, layer re-forming is indicated with these symbols.

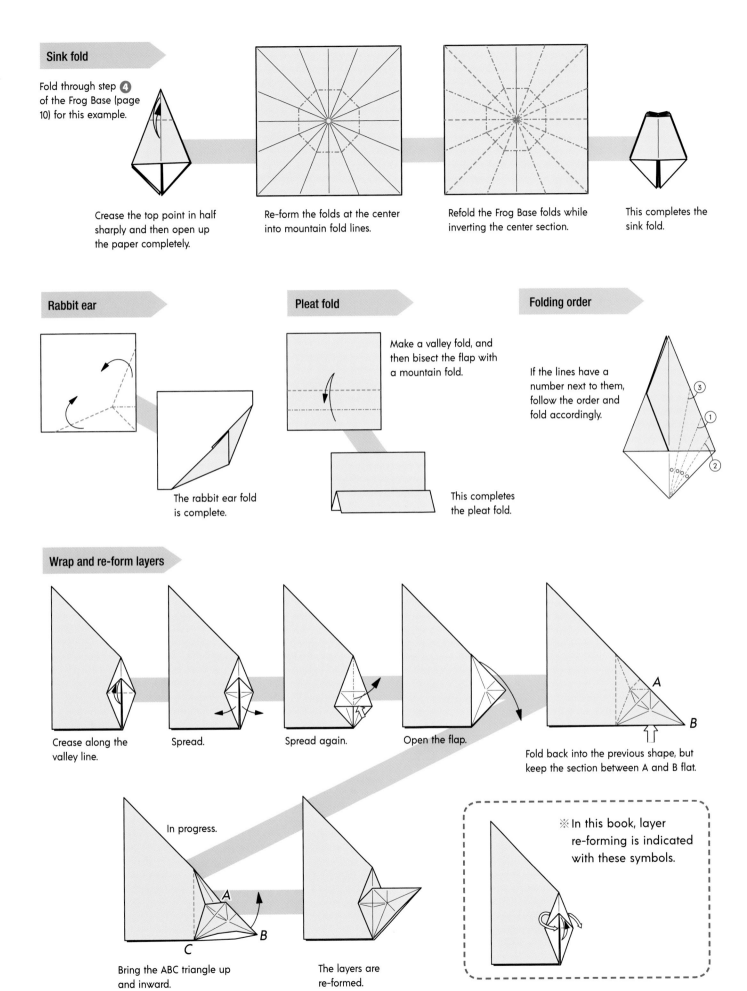

ORIGAMI BASES

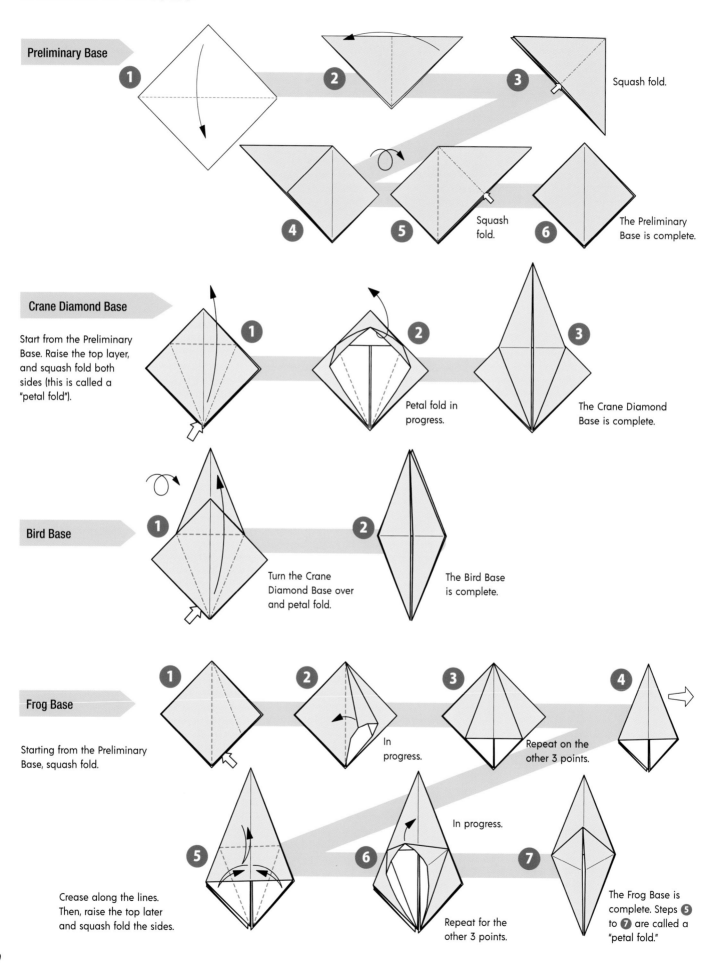

Preliminary Base

1

2

3 Squash fold.

4

5 Squash fold.

6 The Preliminary Base is complete.

Crane Diamond Base

Start from the Preliminary Base. Raise the top layer, and squash fold both sides (this is called a "petal fold").

1

2 Petal fold in progress.

3 The Crane Diamond Base is complete.

Bird Base

1 Turn the Crane Diamond Base over and petal fold.

2 The Bird Base is complete.

Frog Base

Starting from the Preliminary Base, squash fold.

1

2 In progress.

3 Repeat on the other 3 points.

4

5 Crease along the lines. Then, raise the top later and squash fold the sides.

6 In progress. Repeat for the other 3 points.

7 The Frog Base is complete. Steps 5 to 7 are called a "petal fold."

Iris Base

Start from step **4** of the Frog Base. Swing over one layer, and then petal fold. Repeat on the other sides.

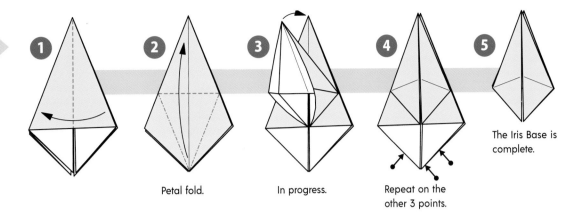

1 **2** **3** **4** **5**

Petal fold.

In progress.

Repeat on the other 3 points.

The Iris Base is complete.

Waterbomb Base

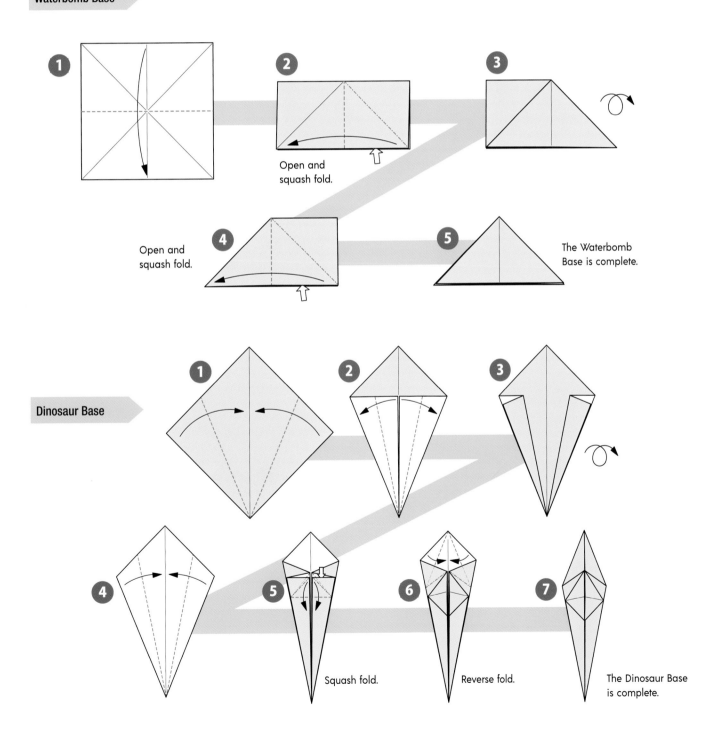

1

2 Open and squash fold.

3

4 Open and squash fold.

5 The Waterbomb Base is complete.

Dinosaur Base

1 **2** **3**

4 **5** Squash fold. **6** Reverse fold. **7** The Dinosaur Base is complete.

HOW TO MAKE LIFELIKE ORIGAMI (USING GLUE)

About Using Glue

One of the keys to making lifelike origami is using craft glue to affect and set the final form. Despite being challenging to do correctly, the finished product will be more realistic and beautiful, as well as strong and durable—so I recommend that you give it a try!

Glue can either be added after the folding is complete or applied incrementally as you fold the origami. (I have added indications in the project instructions for when glue can be applied incrementally). Apply the glue (use slightly diluted craft glue) at the indicated points on the back side of the paper. After the folding is done, add more glue to each fold. Spread glue evenly to bind loose flaps together. However, if there's any sinking or squashing to be done after folding the basic shape, add glue to those parts last (after the sinking or squashing has been accomplished).

If you accidentally put glue in the wrong place, simply wipe it off. Even if it has dried, poorly placed glue can be softened and wiped away after a few minutes by painting the area with a moistened brush.

◀ To prepare the glue solution, slightly dilute some craft glue with water. For application, I suggest you use a 10 mm brush. Also prepare a small water container and a piece of cloth to clean and wipe the brush.

1

Follow the project steps until the text "Start applying glue" is annotated. This is the Octopus (page 98).

2

Slightly spread and open the paper.

3

While being mindful of the creases, apply glue to the correct points on the inside of the model.

4

Fold back to the previous shape.

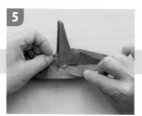

5

While folding back to the previous shape, apply more glue. Remember to only apply glue where necessary.

6

Keep folding back into shape and applying glue until done.

7

Follow the instructions and keep folding.

8

While proceeding, apply more glue when the opportunities arise.

9

Apply glue in tight locations as well, such as the back of the head in this case.

10

After the folding is done, mold the paper into more natural, realistic positions with your fingers.

▼ Glue has been applied

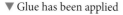

▼ No glue used

Note

Applying glue—while being a very important element in folding lifelike origami—is completely optional. Even just folding is plenty of fun.

ABOUT THE PAPER

Types of Paper and Sizes

For each model, I specifically indicate the type and size of paper that you should use. All of the origami in this book calls for *washi* (Japanese paper, see photo on the right), which has a luxurious weight and texture. There are various types of washi that are easy to fold into several thin layers. In order to produce more beautiful and realistic origami, I recommend using traditional washi with the appropriate strength and stiffness. For applying glue (see previous page), washi is much preferred over standard kami origami paper. Beginners and people who just want to try lifelike origami for fun can, of course, use standard origami paper. For standard origami paper, I generally advise using large sheets (at least 7 x 7 in / 18 x 18 cm or larger).

Preparing the Paper

If you use washi, you can have it cut to size at specialty stores. However, I prefer to cut the washi myself from a large sheet (36 x 24 in / 90 x 60 cm). The size and shape of the sheets changes depending on the folding method used when cutting the large sheet. It can either be cut into 6 or 8 sheets. Once cut to size, prepare multiple Preliminary Bases in advance so they are handy for spur-of-the-moment folding.

Fold a large sheet of paper into sixths.

Cut the folded edges with a craft knife.

The resulting six individual squares.

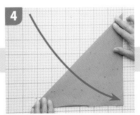
Fold each square into a triangle.

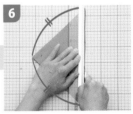
Fold again into a smaller triangle.

Use a craft knife to cut along the long side, in order to straighten the edge.

Only fold the upper layer in a triangle shape. If the corners match perfectly, the cut was successful.

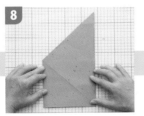
From there, just fold into a Preliminary Base (page 10).

Complete. Store prepared sheets out of direct sunlight.

To display a different color on the back, adhere a second sheet. Use commercially available craft glue diluted with about twice the amount of water. Apply to the paper with a brush, and then overlay and adhere the backing sheet of paper, carefully smoothing any trapped bubbles to the edges.

Strengthen Thin Paper

If your paper is very thin and likely to tear, apply CMC (photo 1: carboxymethylcellulose—available in craft shops) before using. CMC is typically used for leather crafts. For this use, dissolve 1 tablespoon and 1 teaspoon (20 g) of CMC into 2 cups (500 ml) of water and apply it to thin Japanese paper (photo 2).

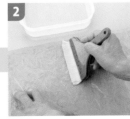

PENGUIN

Type of paper used:

• Handmade Washi (coarse thin white paper
  with black on the reverse)
• 10¼ x 10¼ inch (26 x 26 cm)
• 1 sheet

Folding Tips

I created the Penguin model after receiving specific requests to create a
penguin from students in my origami class. This is a relatively simple
model that starts from the Bird Base. The paper being used here is
white and black washi paper adhered together. Because the folds are
rather simple, the Penguin is easily reproduced using general-purpose
origami paper as well. I recommend using paper that is larger than 8
inches (20 cm). Even if using general-purpose origami paper, the form
of the final product can be stabilized by applying glue, which enables
you to put the model on display indefinitely. It is possible to give the
Penguin different poses, such as one with the wings outstretched or
one with its head lowered to feed a chick. Enjoy experimenting with
these poses. When adjusting its shape, I recommend making the body
3-D by pressing on the mountain crease (on the white back side of the
paper) because this will create a small space between the two feet and
allow the final product to stand independently.

Start from the Bird Base (page 10)

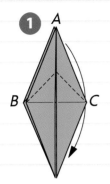
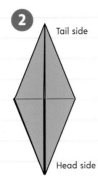
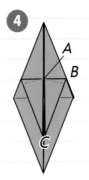
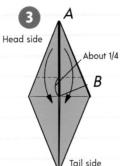
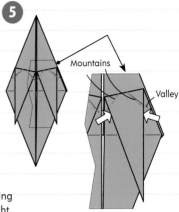

1 Fold the rear flap (ABC) behind.

2 Rotate the paper 180°.

3 Slide the flap up from center point A. The resulting edge BC should lie straight. Repeat on the other side.

Head side / Tail side / About 1/4 / Tail side / Head side

4

5 Reverse fold the two corners. Repeat on the other side.

Mountains / Valley

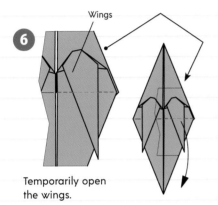
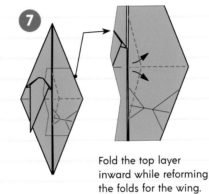
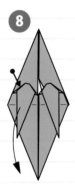

6 Temporarily open the wings.

Wings

7 Fold the top layer inward while reforming the folds for the wing.

8 Repeat steps **6** - **7**.

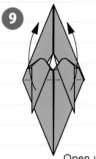
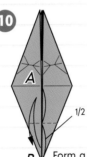
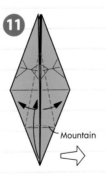

9 Open up the wings.

10 Form a crease about halfway between points A and B.

A / 1/2 / B

11 Fold the top layers outward while squashing the bottop flap up.

Mountain

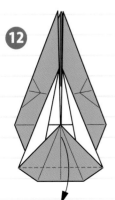
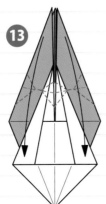

12 Valley fold the flap down.

13 Re-fold the wings.

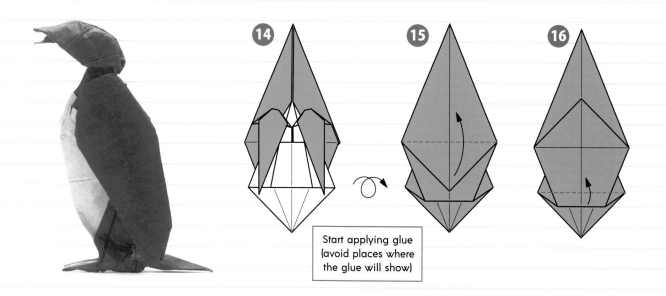

Start applying glue (avoid places where the glue will show)

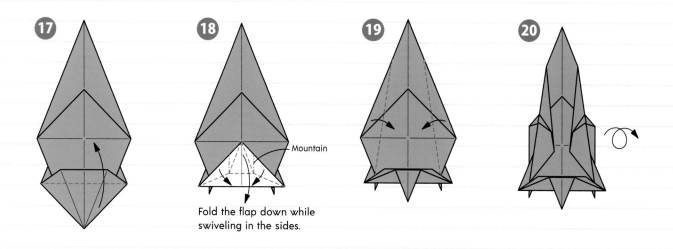

Mountain

Fold the flap down while swiveling in the sides.

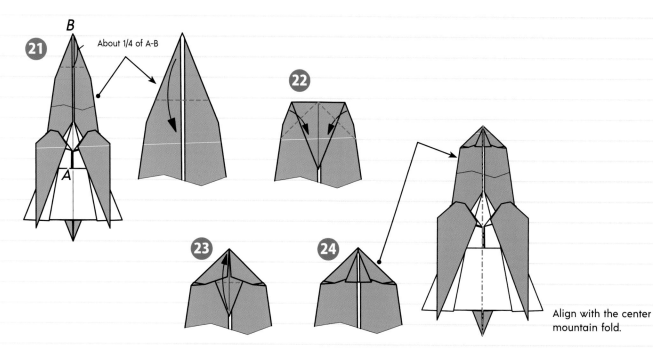

B

About 1/4 of A-B

A

Align with the center mountain fold.

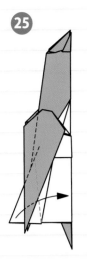

25

Valley fold. Repeat on the other side.

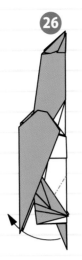

26

Inside reverse fold the center.

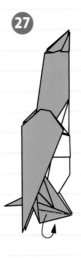

27

Mountain fold the bottom edges inside.

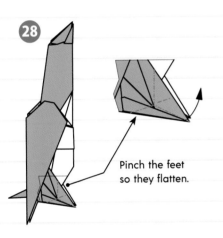

28

Pinch the feet so they flatten.

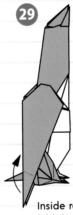

29

Inside reverse fold the tips of the wings.

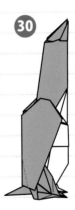

30

Mountain fold the edges of the wings inside.

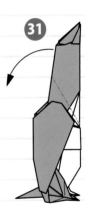

31

Inside reverse fold the center.

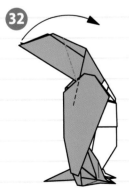

32

Inside reverse fold the center.

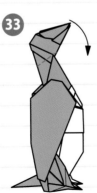

33

Wrap the head flap around and flatten.

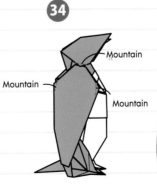

34

Mountain
Mountain
Mountain

35

Fine-tune the shape, and you're done.

DOLPHIN

Type of paper used:
- Handmade Washi
- 9 x 9 inch (23 x 23 cm)
- 1 sheet

Folding Tips

You will begin this model by partially folding the Dinosaur Base. The mountain creases you will make in step 16 will fall into place naturally, but it is a rather complex pattern. The creases you will make in step 12 will facilitate subsequent folds.

Marine mammals such as dolphins, whales, and dugongs have relatively simple bodily structures compared to land mammals, hence the body must be puffed up to create a 3-D look in order to end up with a nicely rounded form. Applying glue will go a long way toward maintaining this form.

While completing step 20, a flap will form in the middle. You can fashion a nice-looking lower jaw by slightly pulling this flap away from the head. Step 26 is where you'll do this.

Start from the Dinosaur Base (page 11), fold through step ⑤

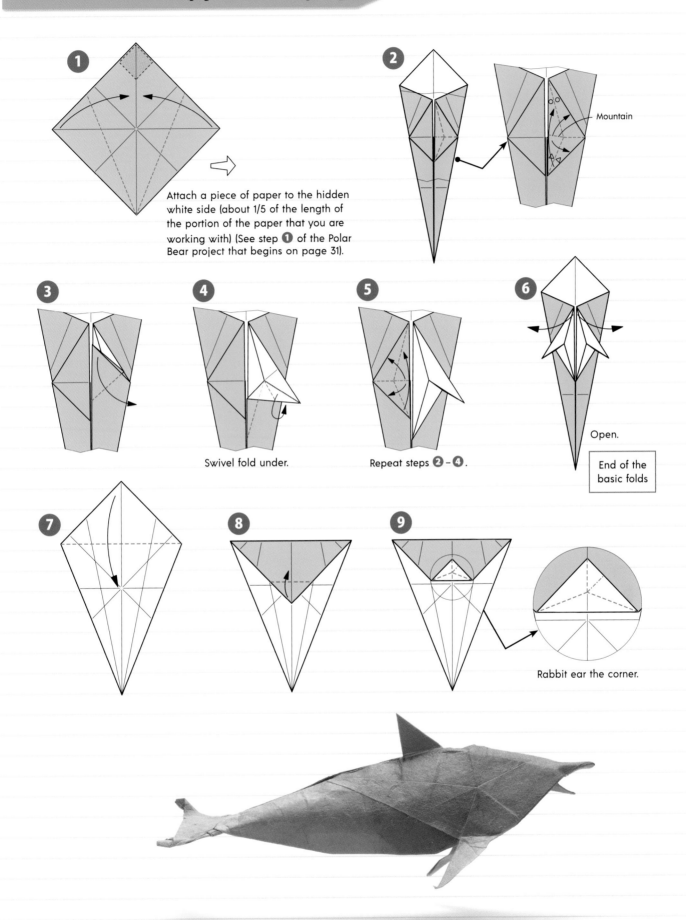

①

Attach a piece of paper to the hidden white side (about 1/5 of the length of the portion of the paper that you are working with) (See step ① of the Polar Bear project that begins on page 31).

② Mountain

③

④ Swivel fold under.

⑤ Repeat steps ②–④.

⑥ Open.

End of the basic folds

⑦

⑧

⑨ Rabbit ear the corner.

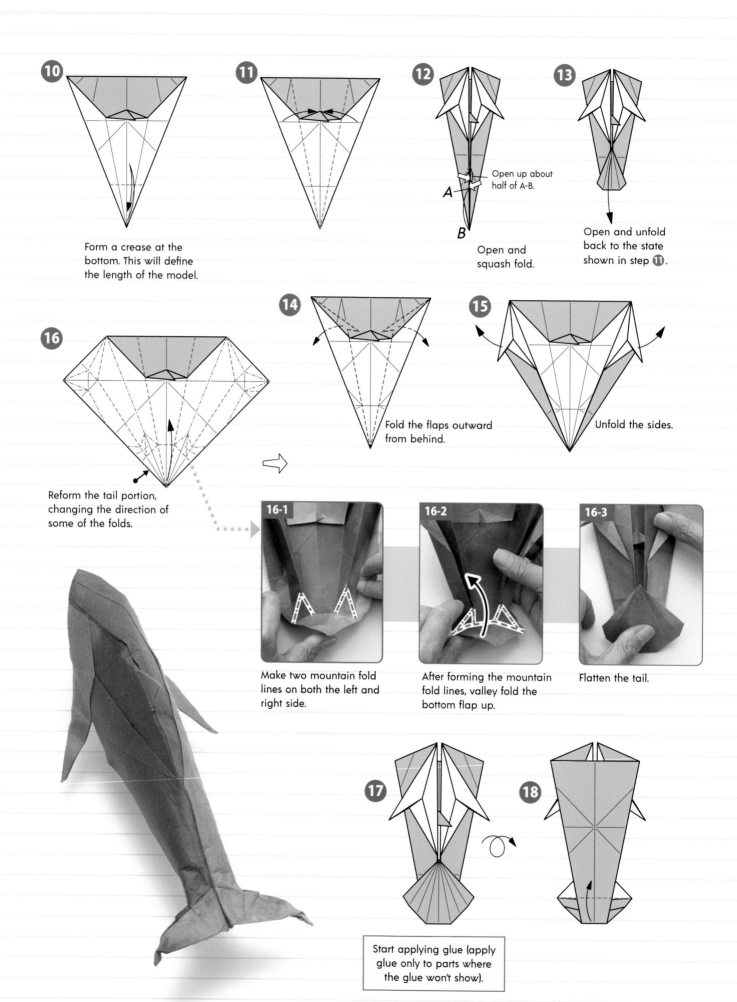

10 Form a crease at the bottom. This will define the length of the model.

11

12 Open and squash fold.

Open up about half of A-B.

A

B

13 Open and unfold back to the state shown in step **11**.

14 Fold the flaps outward from behind.

15 Unfold the sides.

16 Reform the tail portion, changing the direction of some of the folds.

16-1 Make two mountain fold lines on both the left and right side.

16-2 After forming the mountain fold lines, valley fold the bottom flap up.

16-3 Flatten the tail.

17 Start applying glue (apply glue only to parts where the glue won't show).

18

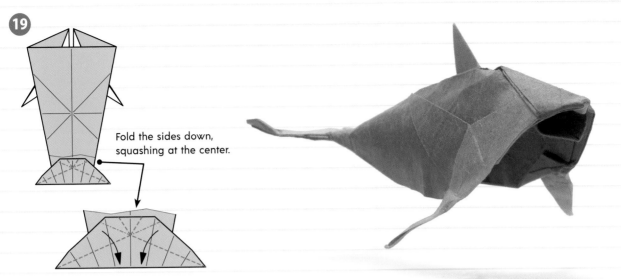

19

Fold the sides down, squashing at the center.

20

Inside reverse fold the sides, petal folding the edge down. The flap that forms will become the jaw.

21

22

Reverse fold the sides up.

23

Valley fold two sets of corners at each side.

24

25

Rabbit ear the corner, tucking the resulting flap inside.

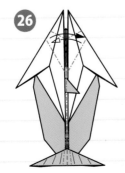

26

Overlap the two top flaps and tuck the tips inside. Open the head portion to make it three-dimensional and shape the tail.

27

Fine-tune the shape, and you're done.

BLUE WHALE CALF

Type of paper used:

- Handmade Washi (pearlescent finish)
- 12¼ x 12¼ inch (31 x 31 cm)
- 1 sheet

Folding Tips

Start folding from the Bird Base. There are two consecutive squash folds from steps 2 to 3, and the dorsal fins are created from the squashed portion. This is similar to the Manta Ray (page 42). The squashed portions become thick, so I recommend that you use thin papers. Because applying glue to the insides after the two consecutive squash folds is difficult, I recommended that you apply glue in advance after the completion of step 4.

For the final adjustments, the body must be rounded. I recommend that you apply glue as a way to maintain this form.

If the lower jaw is opened too widely, the final overall form of the model will lack definition. Although not called for in the instructions, one can add reinforcement (roughly 1/5 the length of the edge to be reinforced) to the portion that will become the lower jaw. See the Polar Bear (page 31) instructions (step 1) for reference.

Start from the Crane Base (page 10)

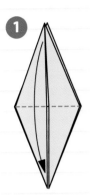

1

Swing down
one flap only.

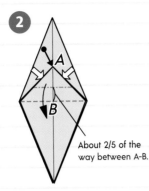

2

A

B

About 2/5 of the
way between A-B.

Squash fold the
center flap.

3

Hidden valley

Squash fold the
side corners.

4

End of the
basic folds

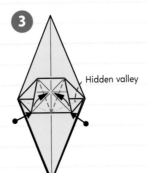

Start applying glue
(glue the back of the parts
squashed in steps **2** and **3**)

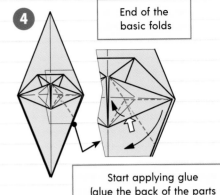

5

6

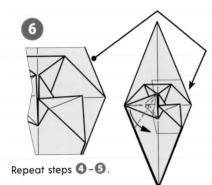

Repeat steps **4**–**5**.

7

8

Swing down one
flap only.

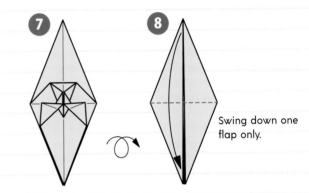

9

Valley fold the upper
flap to the top.

10

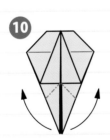

Inside reverse fold
the side flaps.

11

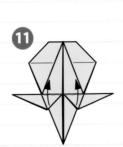

12

Pleat the side flaps.

13

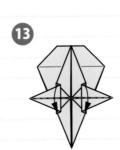

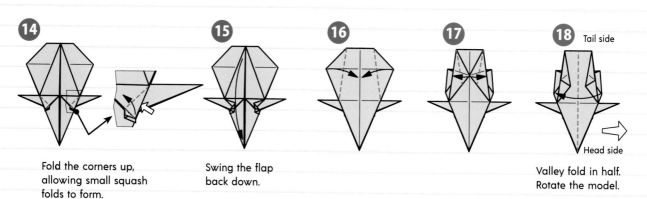

14 Fold the corners up, allowing small squash folds to form.

15 Swing the flap back down.

16

17

18 Tail side / Head side — Valley fold in half. Rotate the model.

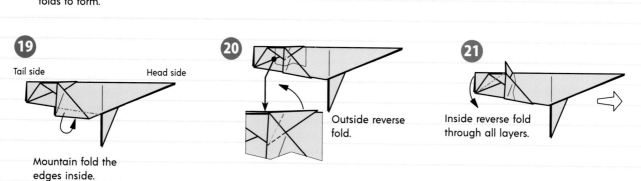

19 Tail side / Head side — Mountain fold the edges inside.

20 Outside reverse fold.

21 Inside reverse fold through all layers.

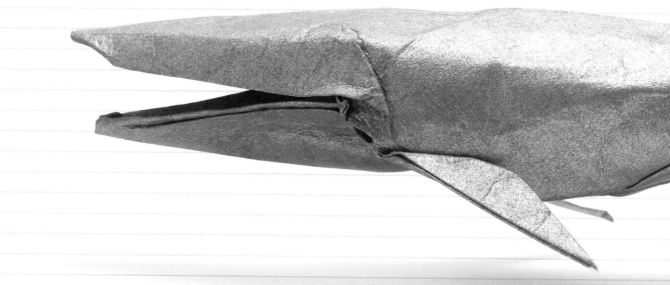

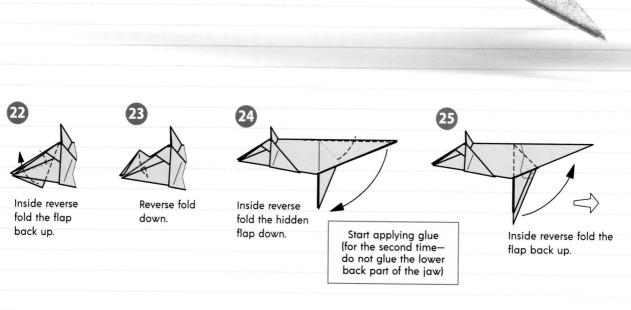

22 Inside reverse fold the flap back up.

23 Reverse fold down.

24 Inside reverse fold the hidden flap down.

Start applying glue (for the second time—do not glue the lower back part of the jaw)

25 Inside reverse fold the flap back up.

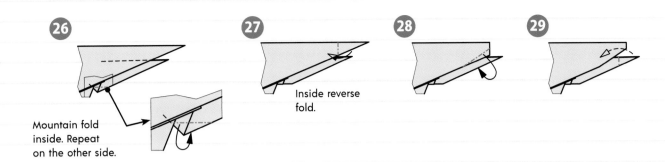

26

Mountain fold inside. Repeat on the other side.

27

Inside reverse fold.

28

29

30

Open out the flap that was just folded and inside reverse fold it.

31

Crimp the sides, making the body three-dimensional.

32

Pleat the fins up.

① Valley
② Mountain

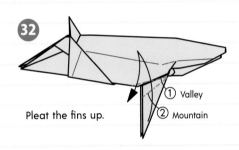

33

Starting from the location indicated by the dot-terminated arrow, open and make the head and body three-dimensional.

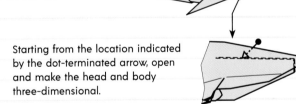

34

Fold the tail with rabbit ear folds.
   Make the body more three-dimensional with mountain fold creases.

35

Fine-tune the shape, and you're done.

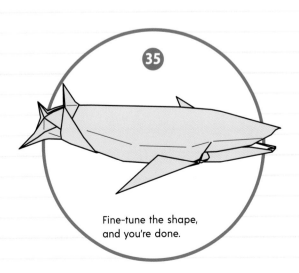

DUGONG

Type of paper used:
- Handmade Washi
- 9 x 9 inch (23 x 23 cm)
- 1 sheet

Folding Tips

The process for folding the tail fin can be applied to other marine animals as well, if one is up for the challenge. In steps 40 and 41, the suggestion of eyes are created by folding two flaps. Be careful not to make the eyes too big.

When using the front fins to adjust the shape, the final form will look better if parts of the body are folded together with the fins. As with the Dolphin (page 18) and Blue Whale Calf (page 22), I recommend that you apply glue to maintain the three-dimensional form.

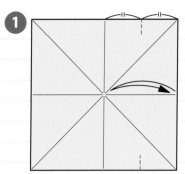

1 Make pinch marks at the halfway point on the right side.

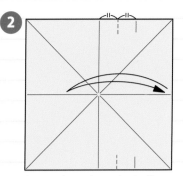

2 Make pinch marks at the halfway point between the middle and the pinch marks made in step **1**.

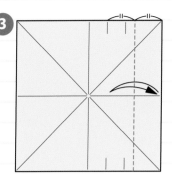

3 Crease the indicated section in half with a valley fold.

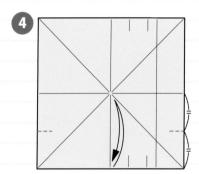

4 Repeat steps **1** – **3** horizontally.

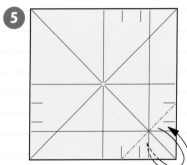

5 Mountain fold and unfold.

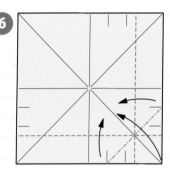

6 Fold the sides in, squashing the corner flat. Rotate the model.

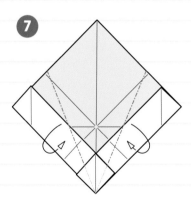

7

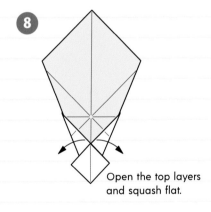

8 Open the top layers and squash flat.

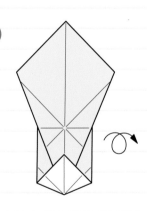

9

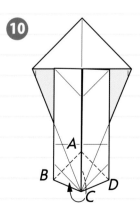

10 Wrap the hidden ABCD flap around to the front.

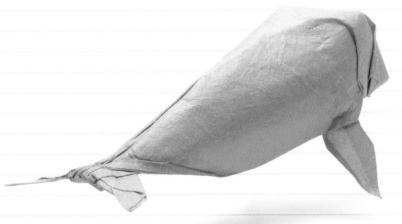

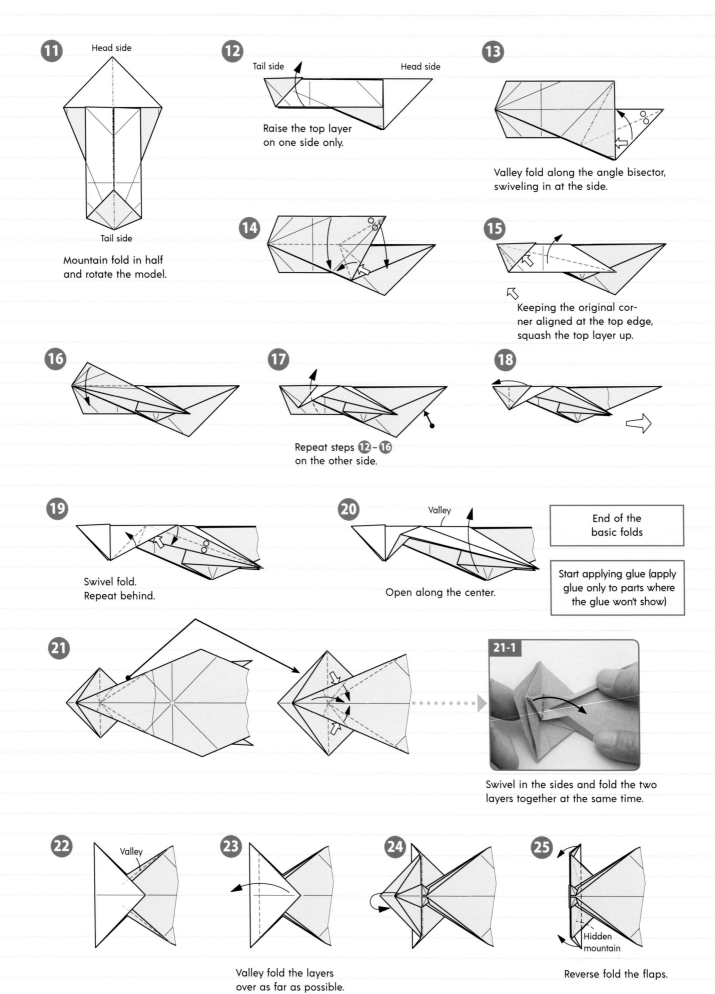

11 Head side

Tail side

Mountain fold in half
and rotate the model.

12 Tail side   Head side

Raise the top layer
on one side only.

13

Valley fold along the angle bisector,
swiveling in at the side.

14

15

Keeping the original cor-
ner aligned at the top edge,
squash the top layer up.

16

17

Repeat steps **12** – **16**
on the other side.

18

19

Swivel fold.
Repeat behind.

20 Valley

Open along the center.

End of the
basic folds

Start applying glue (apply
glue only to parts where
the glue won't show)

21

21-1

Swivel in the sides and fold the two
layers together at the same time.

22 Valley

23

Valley fold the layers
over as far as possible.

24

25

Hidden
mountain

Reverse fold the flaps.

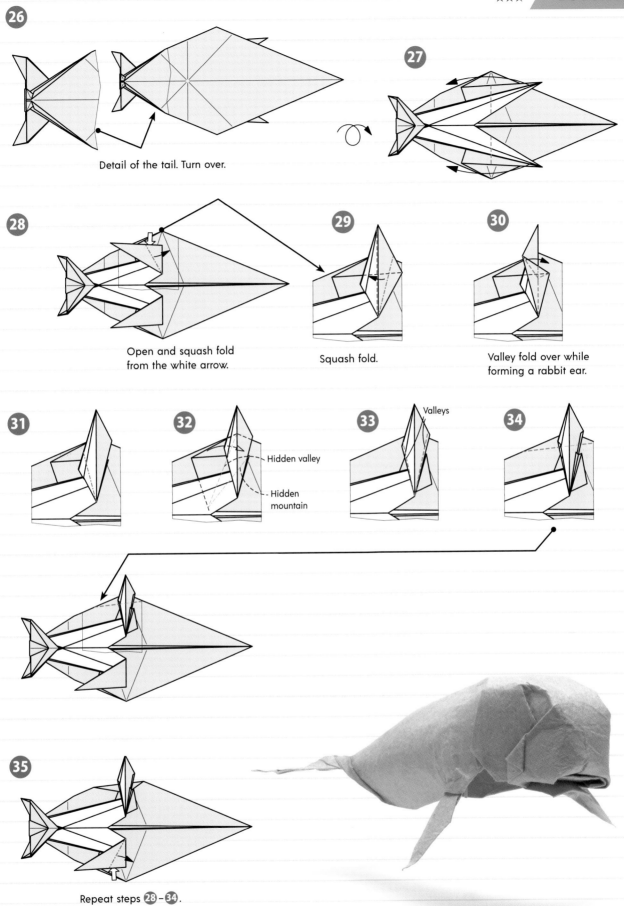

26

Detail of the tail. Turn over.

27

28

Open and squash fold
from the white arrow.

29

Squash fold.

30

Valley fold over while
forming a rabbit ear.

31

32

Hidden valley

Hidden mountain

33

Valleys

34

35

Repeat steps **28** – **34**.

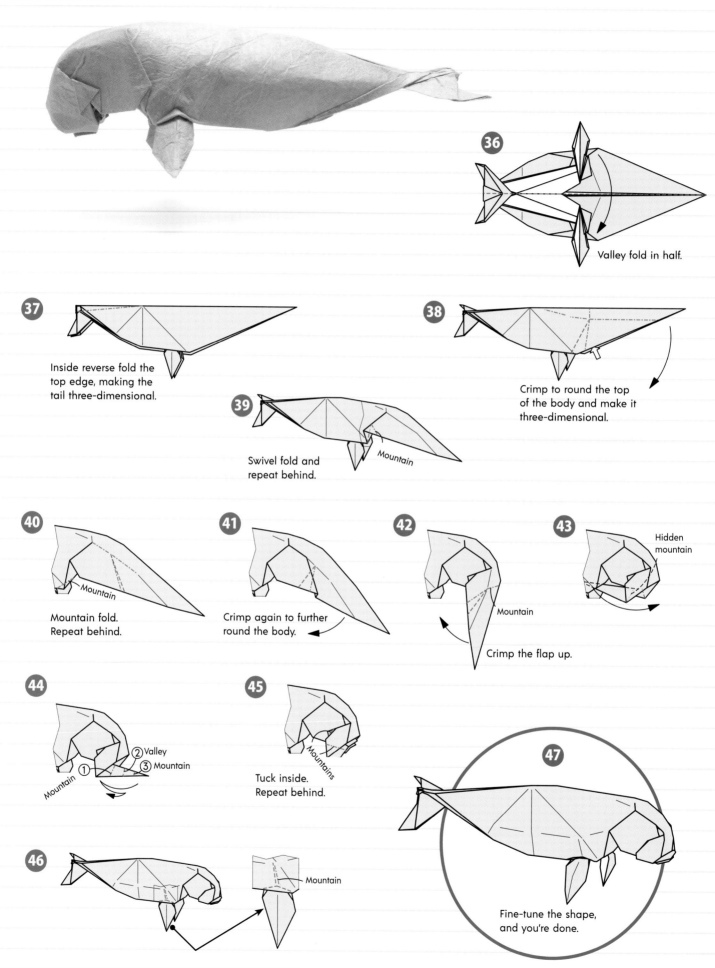

36 Valley fold in half.

37 Inside reverse fold the top edge, making the tail three-dimensional.

38 Crimp to round the top of the body and make it three-dimensional.

39 Swivel fold and repeat behind.

Mountain

40 Mountain fold. Repeat behind.

Mountain

41 Crimp again to further round the body.

42 Crimp the flap up.

Mountain

43 Hidden mountain

44 ① Mountain ② Valley ③ Mountain

45 Tuck inside. Repeat behind.

Mountains

46 Mountain

47 Fine-tune the shape, and you're done.

POLAR BEAR

Type of paper used:
- Handmade Washi
- 12½ x 12½ inch (32 x 32 cm)
- 1 sheet

Folding Tips

I recommend that you reinforce the edges that will become the front legs before you begin folding. For the step-by-step method, refer to the photo-illustrated explanation on page 32. Determine the position of the reinforcing sheet before applying glue, partially spreading it onto the origami paper (not the sheet used for reinforcing). If you accidentally also apply glue onto the reinforcing sheet, the origami paper will become soggy and positioning the reinforcement will be difficult. It's not a problem if some of the glue extends past the edges of the reinforcing sheet; this portion is not visible from the outside of the finished model. This method of adding reinforcement is useful and common, so work to master it. This piece follows a folding method similar to other four-footed creations. Polar bears have relatively long necks, so we'll be reflecting that in this model. Additionally, we'll be making the ears appropriately small, adding some realistic tapering to the legs and paying careful attention to the body shape to give it realistic three-dimensionality.

1

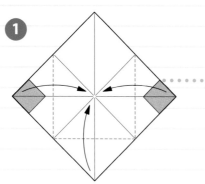

Glue two pieces of reinforcing paper onto the edges of the back side (around 1/5th of the side length each).

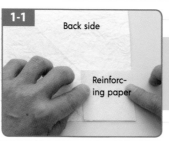

1-1

Align the reinforcing paper with the corner on the back side of the paper. Pin the inside corner with your finger.

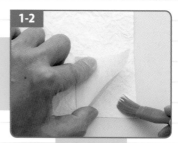

1-2

Peel the square back halfway, and apply glue.

1-3

Peel back the other half of the square and apply glue.

1-4

Smooth the reinforcing paper to remove wrinkles and ensure full contact for a solid bond.

2

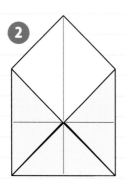

3

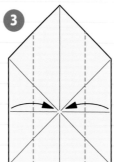

Valley fold the sides to the center, allowing the underlying flaps to swing forward.

4

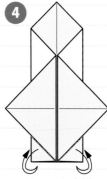

Mountain fold and unfold.

5

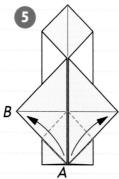

Bring corner A to corner B. Do the same on the other side. Squash flat, allowing the underlying flap to swing forward.

6

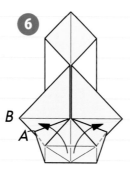

Step **5** in progress.

7

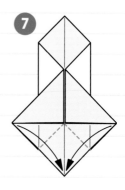

8

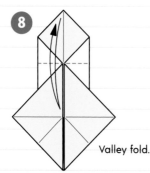

Valley fold.

9

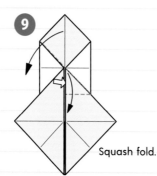

Squash fold.

10

Crease and open out to the state shown in step **8**.

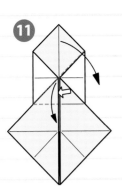

11

Fold the other part in the same way (**9** - **10**) and return to the state shown in step **8**.

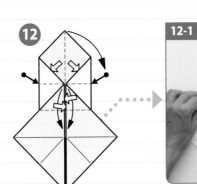

12

12-1

Pull the corners down while squashing the sides flat.

12-2

Close the center flap and pivot to the right.

13

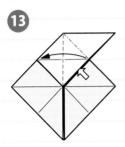

Squash fold.

14

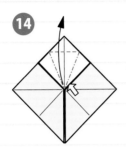

Petal fold.

15

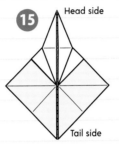

Head side

Tail side

Mountain fold in half and turn the model 90 degrees clockwise.

16

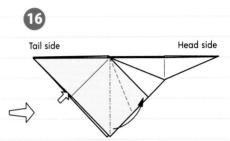

Tail side   Head side

Pull the corner over and squash flat. Repeat behind.

17

18

19

Swivel fold.

20

Fold the other part in the same way (**17** - **19**).

21

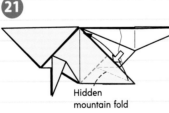

Hidden mountain fold

22

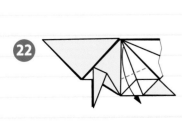

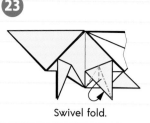

Swivel fold.

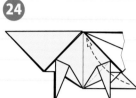

Fold and tuck inside.
Repeat on the other side.

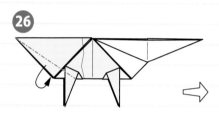

Start applying glue on
the non-visible back
sides, as well as the front
side of the ear and head

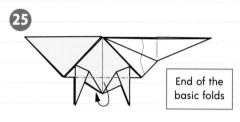

Fold and tuck inside.
Repeat on the other side.

End of the
basic folds

Fold and tuck inside.
Repeat on the other side.

Inside reverse fold.

Swivel in the sides.

Inside reverse fold up.

Mountain

Inside reverse fold.

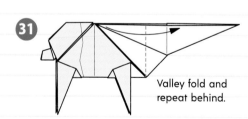

Valley fold and
repeat behind.

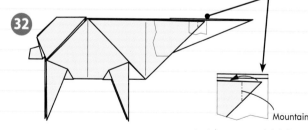

Mountain

Inside reverse fold the
tip. Repeat behind.

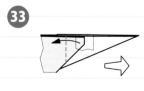

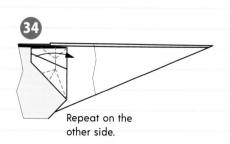

Repeat on the
other side.

Repeat on the
other side.

36

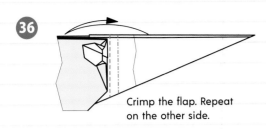

Crimp the flap. Repeat on the other side.

37

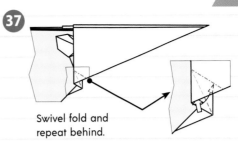

Swivel fold and repeat behind.

38

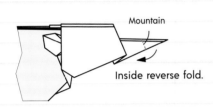

Reverse fold in and then out again.

39

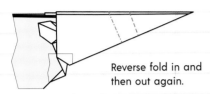

Mountain

Inside reverse fold.

40

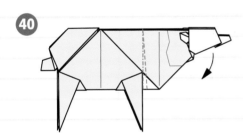

41

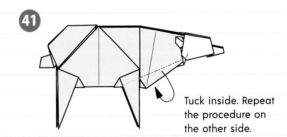

Tuck inside. Repeat the procedure on the other side.

42

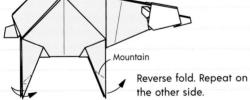

Mountain

Reverse fold. Repeat on the other side.

Heel fold. Repeat on the other side.

43

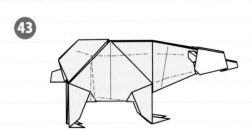

Add mountain fold to make the body three-dimensional.

44

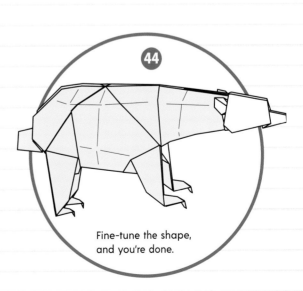

Fine-tune the shape, and you're done.

WALRUS

Type of paper used:
- Handmade Washi
- 12¼ x 12¼ inch (31 x 31 cm)
- 1 sheet

Folding Tips

Reinforcing the front flippers will make the model more sturdy.
Steps 10–13 demonstrate a technique that you will use again when
forming the claws of the Crocodile (page 58), albeit on a much
smaller scale. Step 25 contains a series of photos to show you how to
take the Preliminary Base through its paces. Step 35 features a sink,
which is described in detail at the top of page 9. During step 43,
carefully suggest the shape of each eye when crimp folding to make
the final product look more realistic and three-dimensional.

1

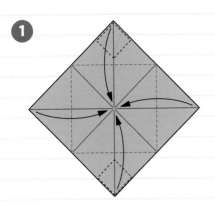

Glue two pieces of reinforcing paper onto the edges of the back side (around 1/5th of the side length each). Refer to Polar Bear (page 31, step **1**).

2

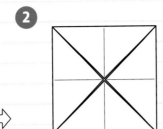

Turn over.

3

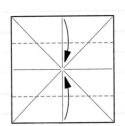

Fold the sides to the center, allowing the flaps to come out from behind.

4

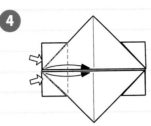

Squash fold the corners.

5

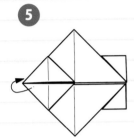

Wrap the flap around from behind and flatten.

6

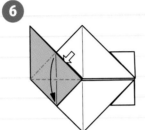

7

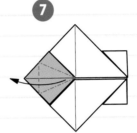

Petal fold (page 10).

8

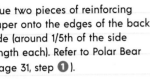

9

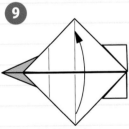

Fold up the one layer.

10

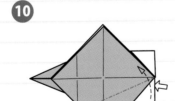

Inside reverse fold along the angle bisector.

11

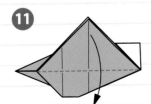

Open in the direction of the arrow and fold.

12

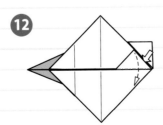

Inside reverse fold.

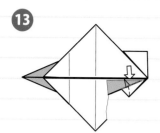

13

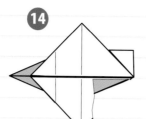

14

15

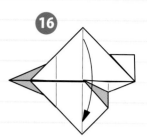

16

The front layer is omitted from steps **13** – **14** for clarity. Inside reverse fold.

Repeat steps **9** – **15** on the top flap.

17

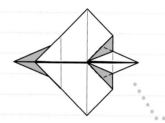

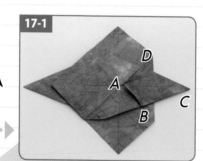

Wrap the back flap around from behind. Turn over first for clarity.

17-1

This photo depicts the diagram in step **17** from the back side. Release the trapped layers of ABCD and invert the flaps.

17-2

The inversion in process. Point C will become concave.

17-3

Push the sides together and push downward.

17-4

Fold the flap down.

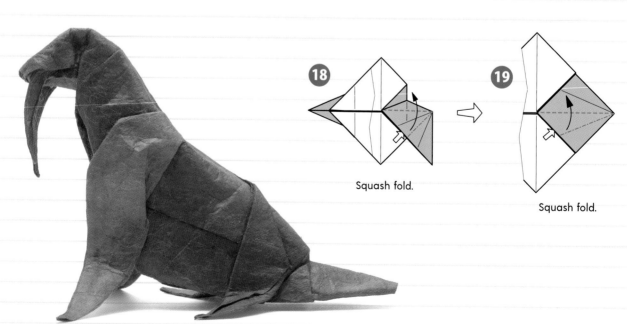

18

Squash fold.

19

Squash fold.

20

21

22

Repeat steps **19**–**21** at the top.

23

Valley fold the top flap.

24

Valley fold the top flaps.

25

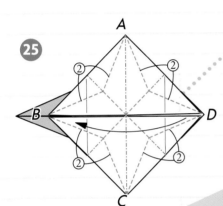

Form square ABCD into a Preliminary Base, and then reverse fold along the lines labeled "2."

25-1

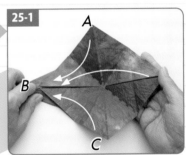

Valley and mountain fold accordingly to fold into a square shape.

25-2

Open up in the direction of the arrow.

25-3

Petal fold.

25-4

Fold.

25-5

Open up the lower flap from 25-2.

25-6

Petal fold.

25-7

Fold.

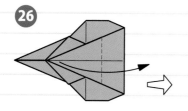

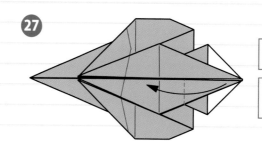

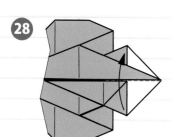

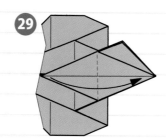

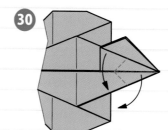

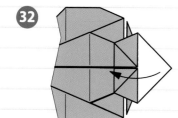

Fold down while reverse folding the flap.

Repeat steps 27 – 30 at the top.

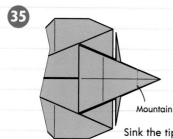

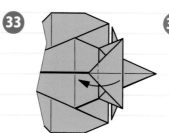

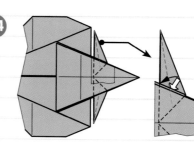

Thin the tusks by valley folding. Fold the other flap and back side in the same way.

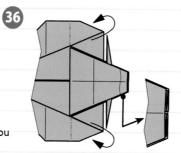

Mountain

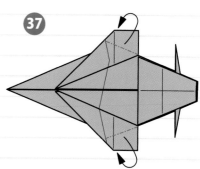

Sink the tip of the flap. You will need to temporarily unfold the side flaps to allow this flap to spread apart.

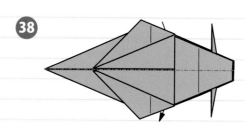

Mountain fold in half. Rotate the model slightly.

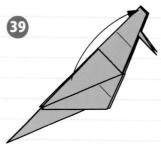

Valley fold and repeat behind.

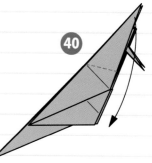

Valley fold and repeat behind.

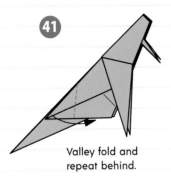

41

Valley fold and repeat behind.

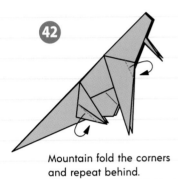

42

Mountain fold the corners and repeat behind.

43

Crimp the head down, leaving a gap from the edge, encouraging it to assume a three-dimensional shape.

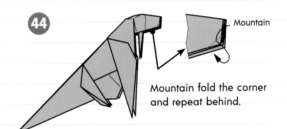

44

Mountain

Mountain fold the corner and repeat behind.

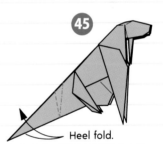

45

Heel fold.

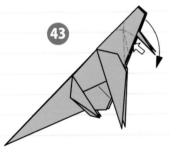

46

Mountain

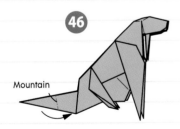

47

Mountain

Mountain

Mountain

Mountain fold the edges and repeat behind. Round out the body with mountain folds.

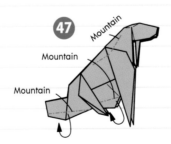

48

Fine-tune the shape, and you're done.

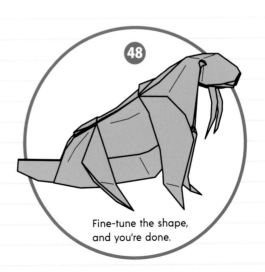

MANTA RAY

Type of paper used:
- Handmade Washi
- 9 x 9 inch (23 x 23 cm)
- 1 sheet

Folding Tips

During a visit to an aquarium, I discovered that manta rays have dorsal fins, and managed to incorporate this into a refined version of my original Manta Ray design. Begin this model by folding the Preliminary Base, and then squash the edges to recreate the pectoral fins. If opting to apply glue, refer to the Blue Whale Calf (page 22) after step 10, spreading the glue on the inner part of the squashed edges. Step 30 is performed in order to keep the tail from pointing downward. Use a pushing motion to modify the angle, but take care not change the shape of the dorsal fin, which should appear at the root of the tail.

Start from the Preliminary Base (page 10)

1

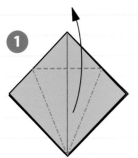

Petal fold the top flap only.

2

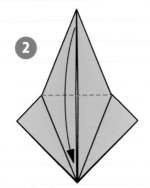

3

2/5th of A-B.

A

B

Squash in the direction of the dot-terminated arrow.

4

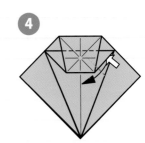

5

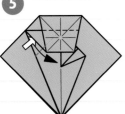

Repeat on the side other side.

6

Hidden valley fold.

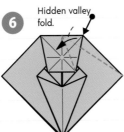

Squash in the direction of the dot-terminated arrow.

7

8

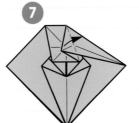

Undo the reverse fold from step **4**.

9

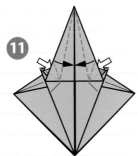

Repeat steps **6** – **8** on the other side.

10

A

B

2/5th of A-B.

End of the basic folds
Start applying glue on the back sides in steps **3** and **6**

11

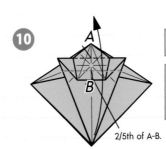

Valley fold the sides in while squashing the corners.

12

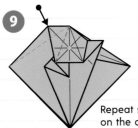

A

B 1/2 of A-B.

Valley fold and unfold.

13

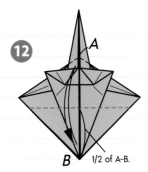

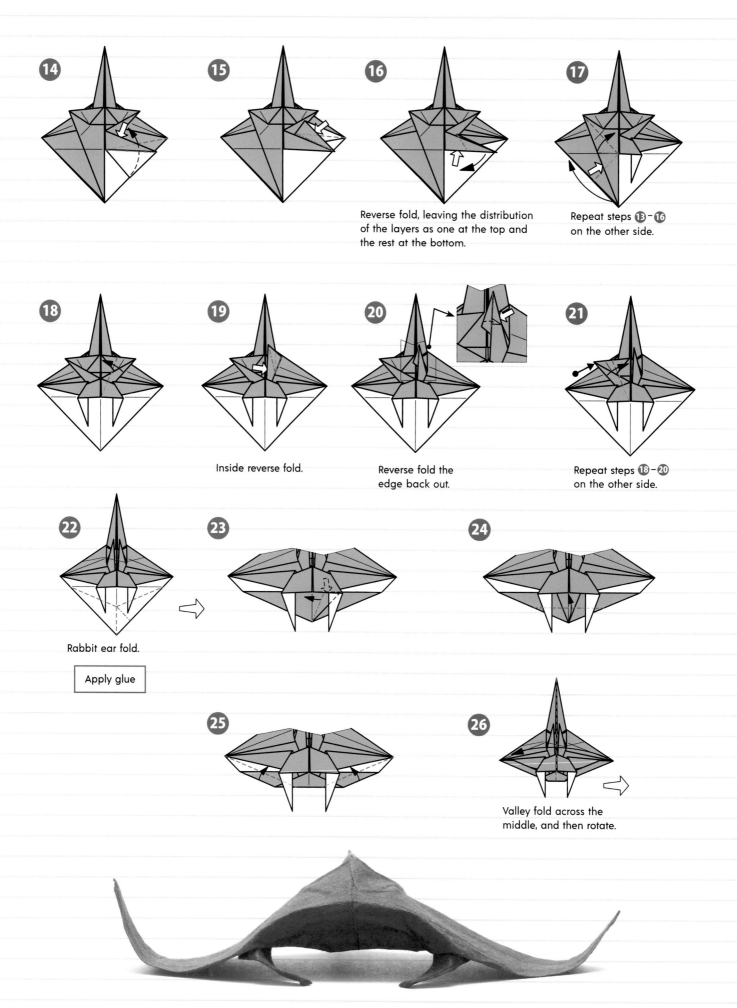

16 Reverse fold, leaving the distribution of the layers as one at the top and the rest at the bottom.

17 Repeat steps 13 – 16 on the other side.

19 Inside reverse fold.

20 Reverse fold the edge back out.

21 Repeat steps 18 – 20 on the other side.

22 Rabbit ear fold.

Apply glue

26 Valley fold across the middle, and then rotate.

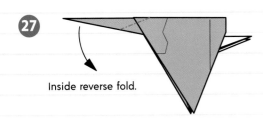

27 Inside reverse fold.

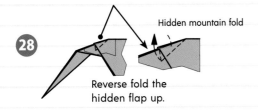

28 Hidden mountain fold

Reverse fold the hidden flap up.

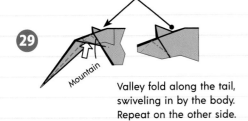

29 Mountain

Valley fold along the tail, swiveling in by the body. Repeat on the other side.

30 Push inside, following the direction of the dot-terminated arrow.

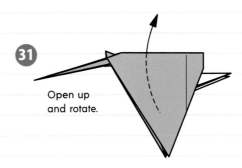

31 Open up and rotate.

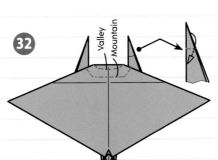

32 Valley Mountain

Inside reverse fold and repeat on the other side.

Mountain fold while paying close attention to the three-dimensional shape.

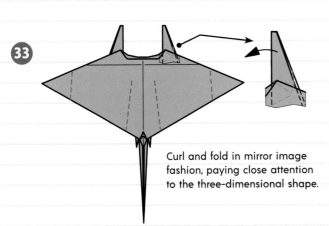

33 Curl and fold in mirror image fashion, paying close attention to the three-dimensional shape.

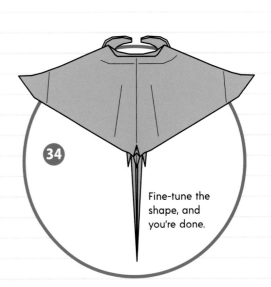

34 Fine-tune the shape, and you're done.

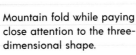

SWORDFISH

Type of paper used:
• Handmade Washi
• 9 x 9 inch (23 x 23 cm)
• 1 sheet

Folding Tips

Refer to the Waterbomb Base instructions (page 11) when starting this model, which is relatively simple compared to others in the book. Step 18 requires a valley fold across the middle, causing the back to be visibly open. This is not ideal, but it's necessary in order to make the folding procedure much simpler. In this book, the Goldfish (page 54) and the Penguin (page 14) also apply this technique. Step 22 is performed by reverse folding the second dorsal fin. When it comes to applying glue, I recommend that you start after step 22, returning the structure back to the state of step 11 as you apply glue to hidden surfaces and refold. In the case of fish, apply mountain folds to add volume to the body of the fish to make the final product look more three-dimensional. Mountain folding the upper jaw and opening up the lower jaw will result in an angular, kinetic look.

Start from the Waterbomb Base (page 11)

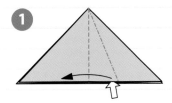

1

Open in the direction of the white arrow and squash fold.

2

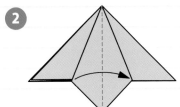

3

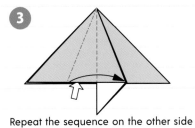

Repeat the sequence on the other side to make the model symmetrical.

4

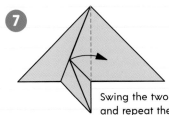

Petal fold.

5

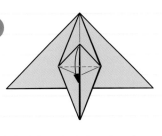

Swing two flaps over.

6

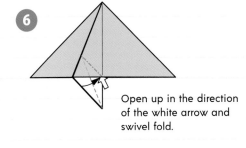

Open up in the direction of the white arrow and swivel fold.

7

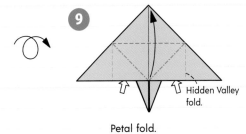

Swing the two flaps back and repeat the sequence on the other side to make the model symmetrical.

8

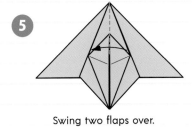

9

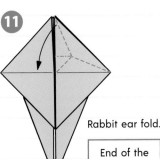

Hidden Valley fold.

Petal fold.

10

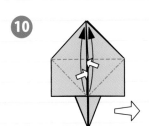

Squash fold the flaps up.

11

Rabbit ear fold.

End of the basic folds

12

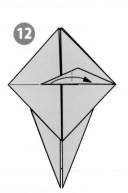

13

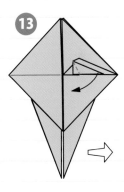

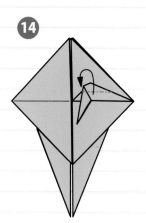

14

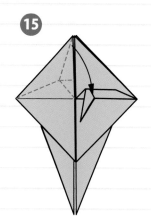

15

Repeat steps **11** - **14** on the other side.

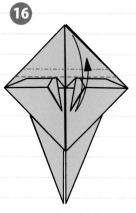

16

Pleat fold.

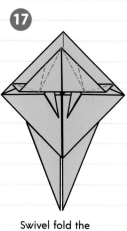

17

Swivel fold the sides behind.

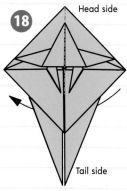

18

Head side

Tail side

Mountain fold across the middle and rotate.

19

Tail side

Head side

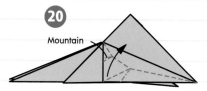

20

Mountain

Fold the flap up and swivel in the sides.

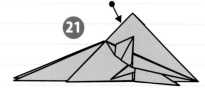

21

Repeat steps **19** - **20** behind.

22

Hidden mountain fold

Reverse fold the hidden center flap up.

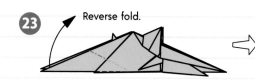

23

Reverse fold.

Start applying glue on the non-visible back sides

24

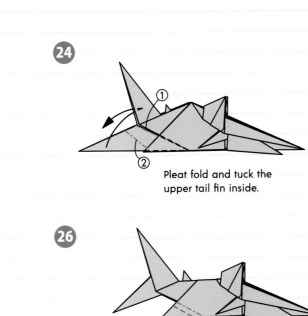

①
②

Pleat fold and tuck the
upper tail fin inside.

25

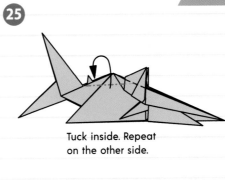

Tuck inside. Repeat
on the other side.

26

Crimp and tuck inside.
Repeat on the other side.

27

Mountain

Squash in the direction of
the dot-terminated arrow
and open up the mouth.

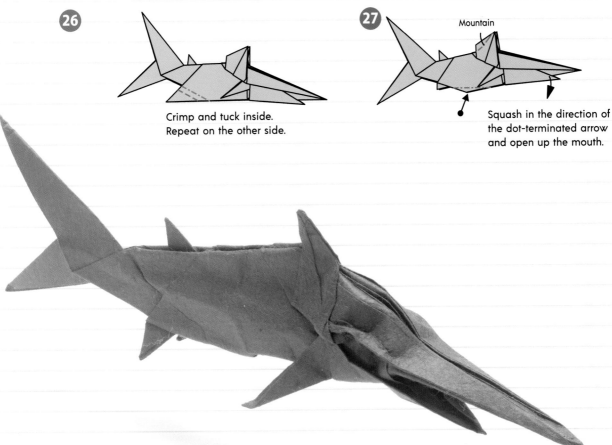

28

Mountain

Squash in the direction of the
dot-terminated arrows. Apply
mountain folds to add volume
to the body of the fish for a
three-dimensional effect.

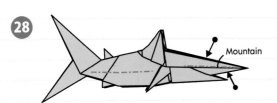

29

Fine-tune the shape,
and you're done.

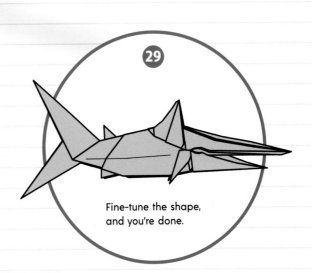

SEAHORSE

▶ Difficulty: ★★★

Type of paper used:
- Handmade Washi
- 9 x 9 inch (23 x 23 cm)
- 1 sheet

Folding Tips

The dorsal fin details will be precreased at the outset. When completing the dorsal fin at step 9, it is important to apply glue thoroughly to preserve the shape. However, step 22 will require further small folds to the dorsal fin, so do not apply glue to the inner face. The fold at step 18 is a little unusual, but it is performed by making an indent with your fingernails, while alternating mountain and valley folds on both sides. This allows for the creation of a curving scalloped line, typical of a seahorse's back. When applying glue, note that the final product will look much more polished if you apply glue to all of the tiny folds as well. As a final step, adding some volume to the body will result in a three-dimensional look.

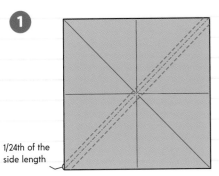

1 Alternate mountain and valley folds. See page 59 for an example of how to locate 1/24th of an edge.

1/24th of the side length

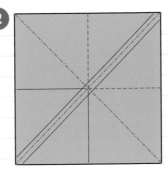

2 Form a Waterbomb Base with one flap swung to the other side.

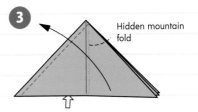

3 Hidden mountain fold

Open up in the direction of the white arrow and valley fold, squashing the middle flap over to the left.

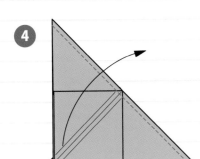

4

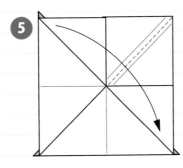

5

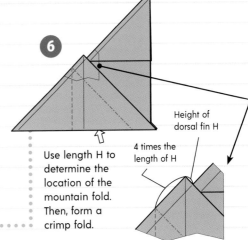

6 Hidden mountain fold

Height of dorsal fin H

4 times the length of H

Use length H to determine the location of the mountain fold. Then, form a crimp fold.

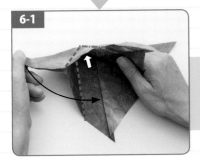

6-1 Open up the sheet and fold.

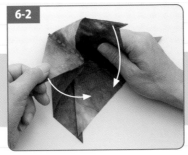

6-2 Valley fold in the direction of the arrows.

6-3 The paper after folding.

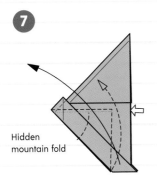

7 Hidden mountain fold

Open up in the direction of the white arrow and squash fold the middle flap.

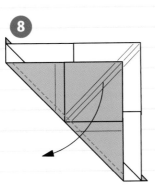

8

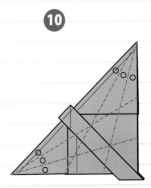

9 Start applying glue, excluding the back side of the dorsal fin

10 Alternate mountain and valley folds. Repeat on the other side.

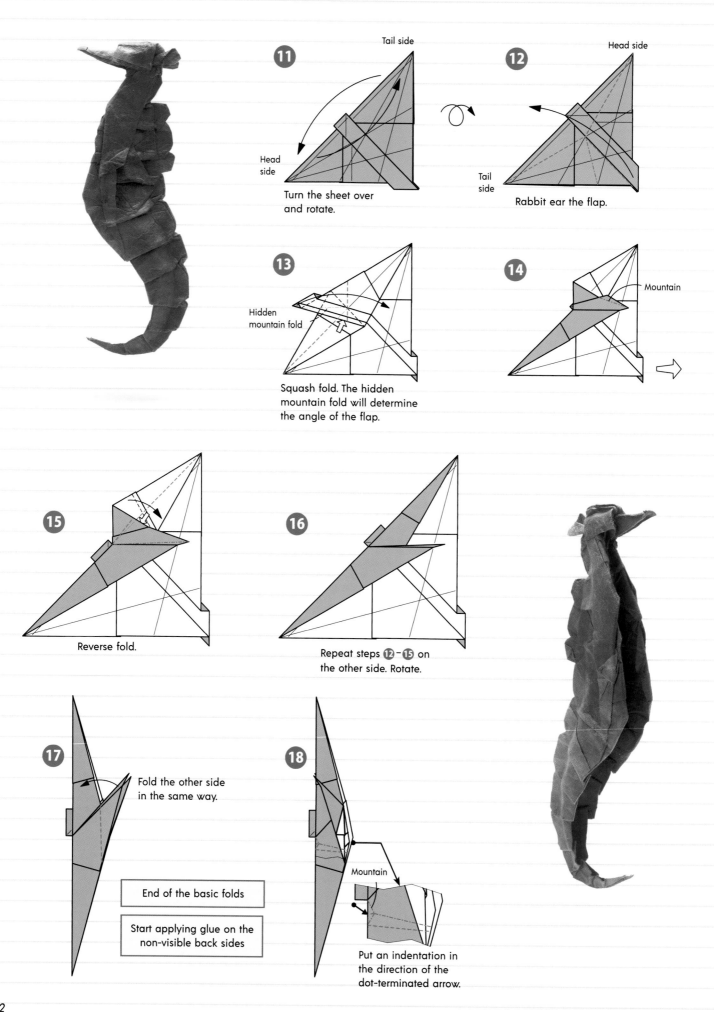

11 Turn the sheet over and rotate.

Tail side

Head side

12 Rabbit ear the flap.

Head side

Tail side

13 Squash fold. The hidden mountain fold will determine the angle of the flap.

Hidden mountain fold

14 Mountain

15 Reverse fold.

16 Repeat steps **12** – **15** on the other side. Rotate.

17 Fold the other side in the same way.

End of the basic folds

Start applying glue on the non-visible back sides

18 Mountain

Put an indentation in the direction of the dot-terminated arrow.

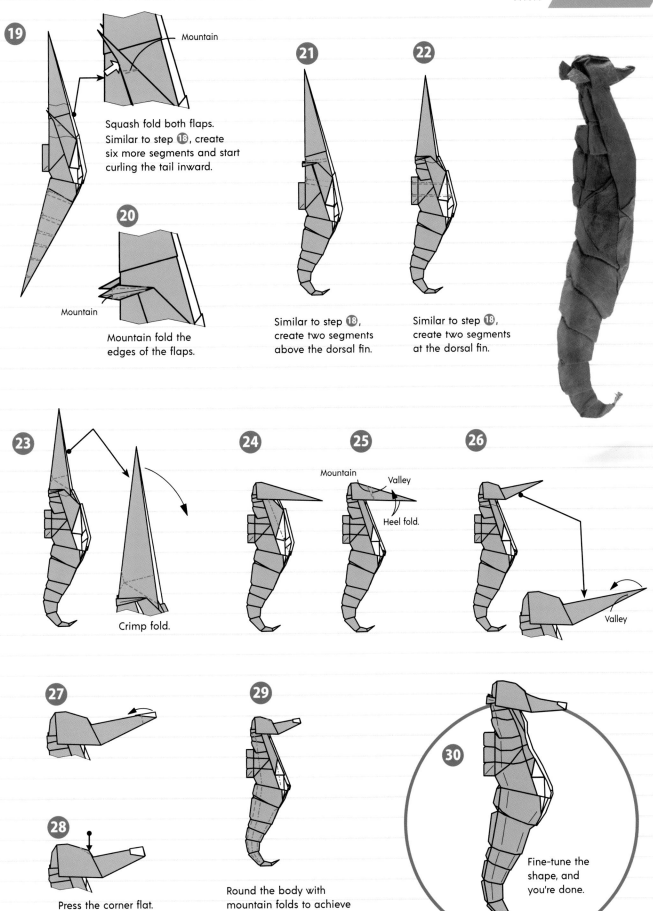

19

Mountain

Squash fold both flaps. Similar to step **18**, create six more segments and start curling the tail inward.

20

Mountain

Mountain fold the edges of the flaps.

21

Similar to step **18**, create two segments above the dorsal fin.

22

Similar to step **18**, create two segments at the dorsal fin.

23

Crimp fold.

24

25

Mountain

Valley

Heel fold.

26

Valley

27

28

Press the corner flat.

29

Round the body with mountain folds to achieve a three-dimensional look.

30

Fine-tune the shape, and you're done.

GOLDFISH

Type of paper used:
- Handmade Washi
- 9 x 9 inch (23 x 23 cm)
- 1 sheet

Folding Tips

This model is fashioned after the fantail goldfish. Similar to the Swordfish (page 46), the back is visibly open. Step 14 is performed to create large fins. This method is not particularly difficult, but I added some photos for guidance, as the three-dimensional shape is important. When splitting the fins in step 22, valley folding the back will enhance the shape. When finishing this piece, use either cotton or crumpled tissue to fill the body to give it three-dimensionality. I recommend applying glue throughout the back, and allowing it to dry before filling it to maintain the original form of the model.

Start from the Dinosaur Base (page 11)

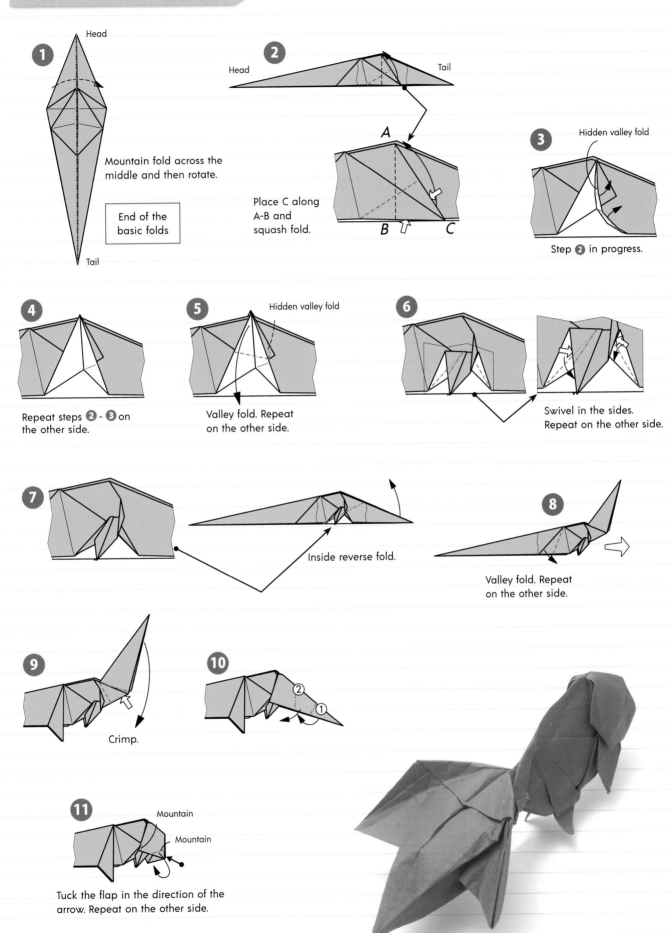

1 Head

Mountain fold across the middle and then rotate.

End of the basic folds

Tail

2 Head   Tail

A

Place C along A-B and squash fold.

B   C

3 Hidden valley fold

Step **2** in progress.

4 Repeat steps **2** - **3** on the other side.

5 Hidden valley fold

Valley fold. Repeat on the other side.

6 Swivel in the sides. Repeat on the other side.

7 Inside reverse fold.

8 Valley fold. Repeat on the other side.

9 Crimp.

10

11 Mountain

Mountain

Tuck the flap in the direction of the arrow. Repeat on the other side.

12 Inside reverse fold.

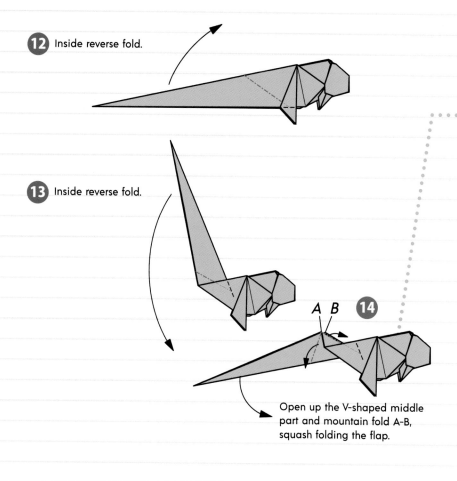

13 Inside reverse fold.

A B **14**

Open up the V-shaped middle part and mountain fold A-B, squash folding the flap.

15

Hidden mountain fold

B

A

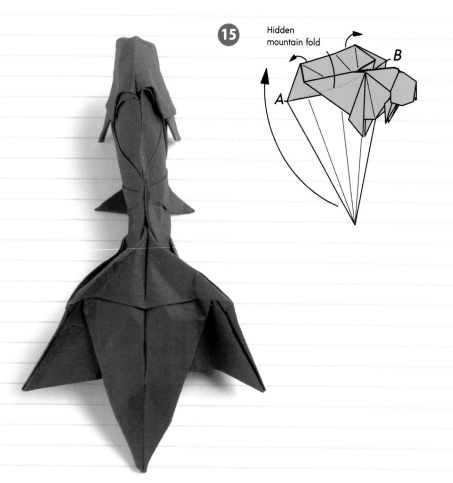

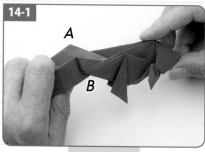

14-1

A

B

Insert a finger or thumb from the bottom.

14-2

A

B

Mountain fold A-B.

14-3

A

B

Tilt the tip of the fin downward.

14-4

A

B

Fold.

14-5

Step **14**, complete.

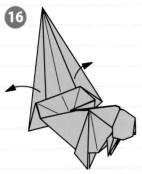
16

Open out the trapped
layers at each side.

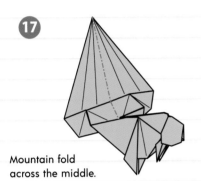
17

Mountain fold
across the middle.

Start applying glue on
the non-visible back sides

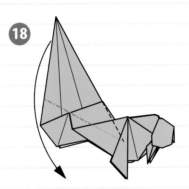
18

Inside reverse fold.

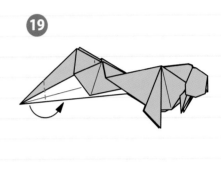
19

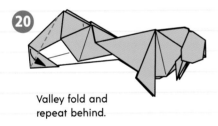
20

Valley fold and
repeat behind.

21

Hidden mountain fold

① Mountain

② Valley

22

Hide with a mountain fold and
repeat behind. Valley fold while
opening up the fin.

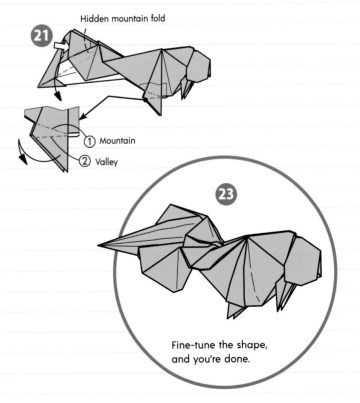
23

Fine-tune the shape,
and you're done.

CROCODILE

Type of paper used:
- Handmade Washi
- 12¼ x 12¼ inch (31 x 31 cm)
- 1 sheet

Folding Tips

This creation requires the application of a 24-division pleat fold. First, you'll make creases to divide the sheet into thirds. This is explained in detail in steps 1–3, but you can also judge it by eye. After the sheet has been divided into three both horizontally and vertically, add another 4 divisions by accordion folding to complete this crease pattern. This step is explained in detail on step 17 using a series of photos, so refer to this step when necessary. Pay particular attention to the details in steps 14 and 15, as precision there is critical. Step 27 is performed to make the body look three-dimensional. Shift the two valley folds closest to the middle, and pull in the closest mountain fold to the middle to achieve this.

The realism of this model can be further enhanced by paying close attention to the details of the structure around the eyes.

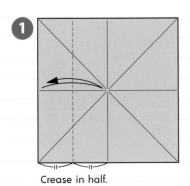

1 Crease in half.

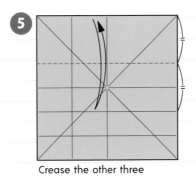

2 Form a crease that passes through point A.

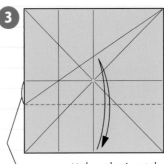

3 Make a horizontal crease starting from the lower end of the crease from step **2**.

1/6th of the length of the sides.

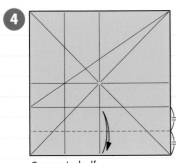

4 Crease in half.

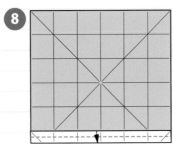

5 Crease the other three parts in the same way.

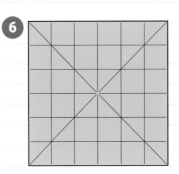

6

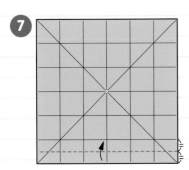

7

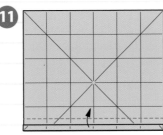

8

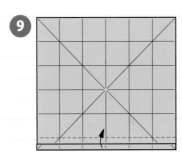

9

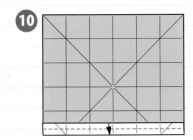

10

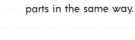

11 In this way (**7**–**10**), continue folding to the middle.

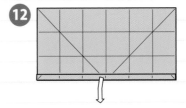

12

13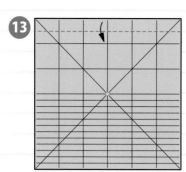

Fold the other three sections in the same way (**8** – **12**).

14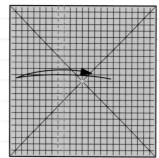

Pleat fold the fourth valley fold from the middle on the left and the third mountain fold from the middle on the left.

15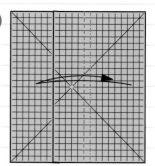

Pleat fold the second valley fold from the middle on the right and the third mountain fold from the middle on the right.

16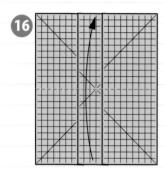

17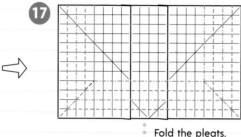

Fold the pleats.

17-1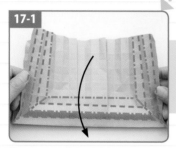

Illustration of the folding process.

17-2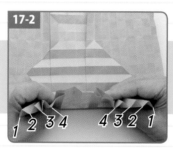

Four corners appear on either end of the bottom edge. Continue folding.

17-3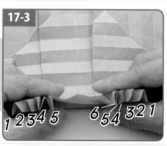

There now should be 5 corners on the left side and 6 on the right.

17-4

Mountain fold the fifth corner from the right at a 45 degree angle.

17-5

Likewise, mountain fold the fifth corner from the left at a 45 degree angle.

17-6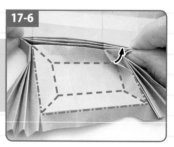

Pull one pleat over to the right and flatten. Sink the middle section.

17-7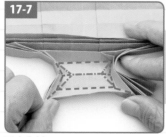

Sink fold.

17-8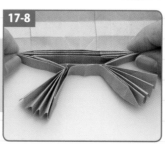

The structure after folding.

18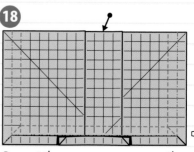

Repeat the same sequence on the other side.

19

Squash fold the four corners

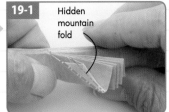

19-1 Hidden mountain fold

Mountain fold twice.

19-2

The structure after the mountain fold.

19-3

Valley fold.

19-4

The structure after the valley fold.

20

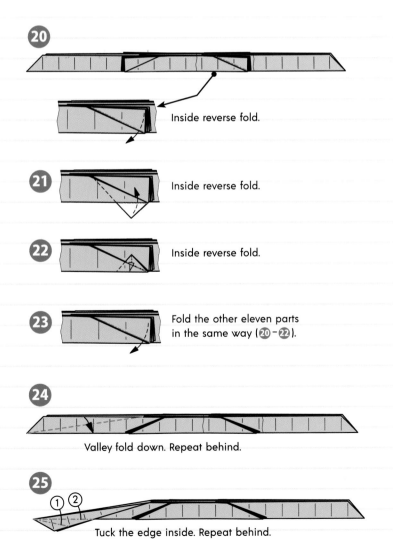

Inside reverse fold.

21 Inside reverse fold.

22 Inside reverse fold.

23 Fold the other eleven parts in the same way (**20** - **22**).

24

Valley fold down. Repeat behind.

25

① ②

Tuck the edge inside. Repeat behind.

26

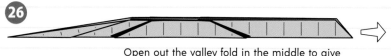

Open out the valley fold in the middle to give
the body a three-dimensional look.

27

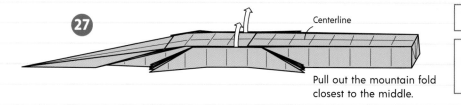

Centerline

Pull out the mountain fold
closest to the middle.

28

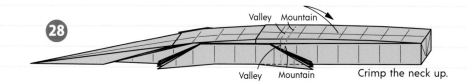

Valley   Mountain

Valley   Mountain

Crimp the neck up.

29

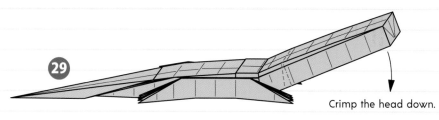

Crimp the head down.

30

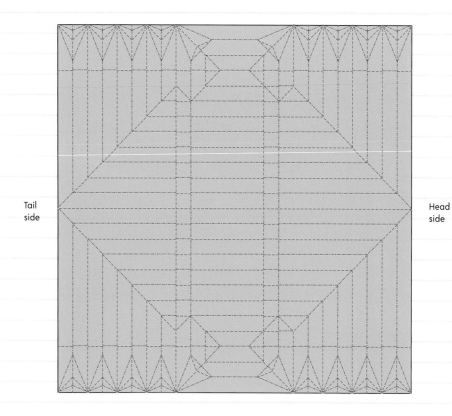

Flatten the front edge into a point
while crimping the sides.

The Crocodile crease pattern   (※ through step **24**)

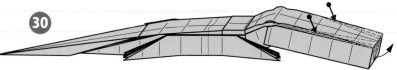

Tail
side

Head
side

31

32

Tuck in. Repeat on
the other side.

33

Valley fold. Repeat
on the other side.

34

Valley fold, allowing tiny
squash folds to form.

35

Mountain ① 　　 Open up five claws.
② Valley

36

Do the same with the
other three legs (**34**–**35**).

37

Fine-tune the shape,
and you're done.

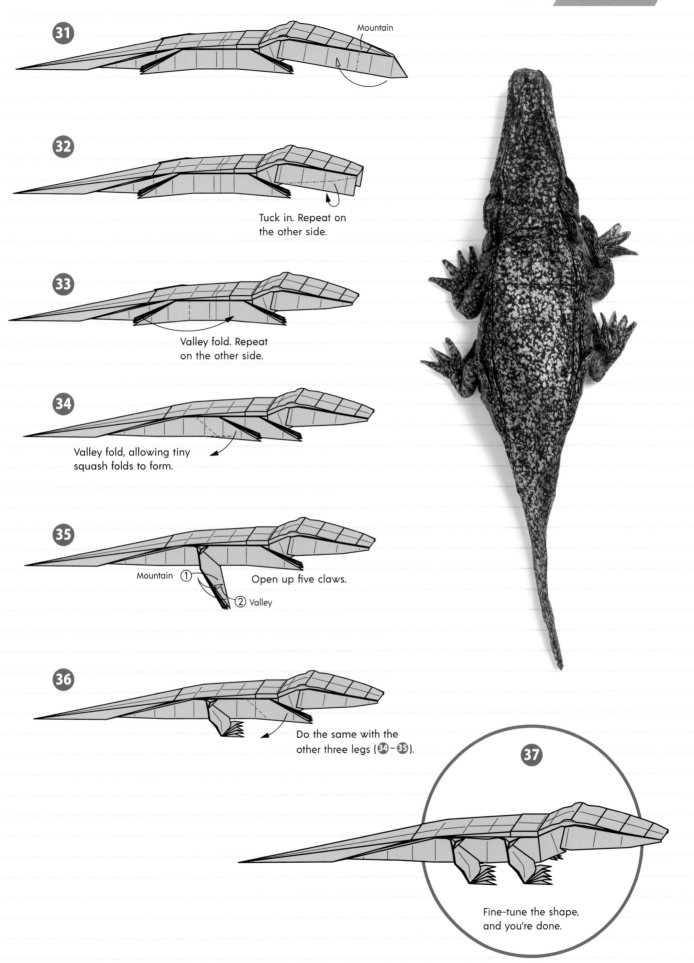

ELASMOSAURUS

Type of paper used:
- Handmade Washi
- 10¼ x 10¼ inch (26 x 26 cm)
- 1 sheet

Folding Tips

Among the many plesiosaurs, the Elasmosaurus possesses one of the longest necks. Frankly, this creation reminds one more of the Futabasaurus due to the shorter neck length. The basic folds pattern of this piece is unique, which I hope you will enjoy. Initially, I devised this method to fold long-necked turtles, but I adjusted it for this prehistoric application. The reverse fold at step 18 allows you to tuck in the excess edge at the middle part of the neck.

You will be prompted to start applying glue at step 26, but you will want to unfold a few steps (for instance, back to step 20) before applying glue and returning the model to the step-26 state again.

Generally speaking, this is good practice every time you're prompted to start applying glue.

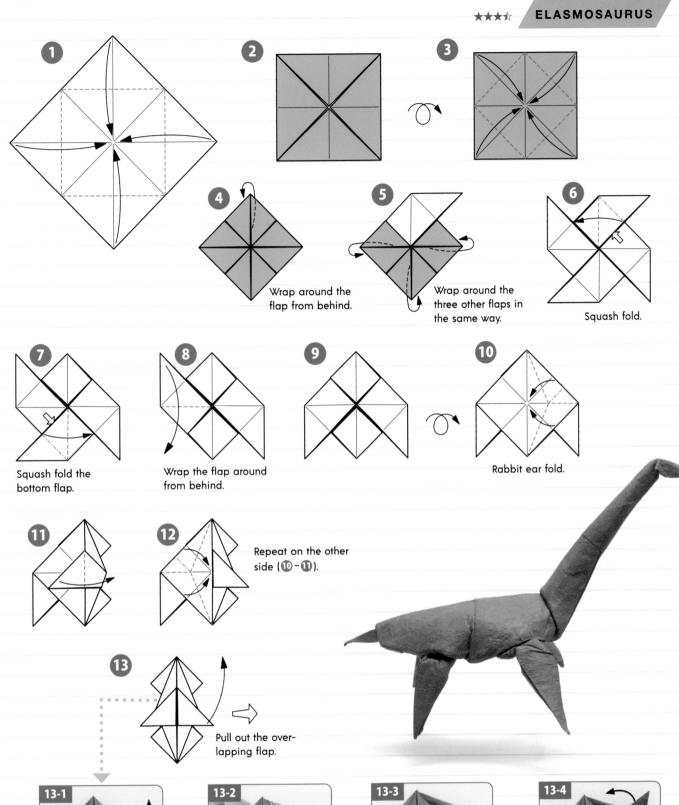

1

2

3

4
Wrap around the flap from behind.

5
Wrap around the three other flaps in the same way.

6
Squash fold.

7
Squash fold the bottom flap.

8
Wrap the flap around from behind.

9

10
Rabbit ear fold.

11

12
Repeat on the other side (**10**–**11**).

13
Pull out the overlapping flap.

13-1

Pull out the overlapping flap.

13-2

The three sections should be equal.

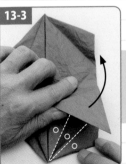

13-3

Likewise, the three sections on the bottom side should be equal.

13-4

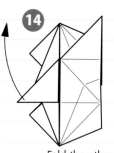

Fold the other side
in the same way.

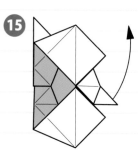

Rear view of step **14**.

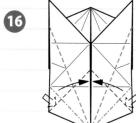

Pleat the sides along the existing
creases, squash folding flat.

Fold 1, and
then 2.

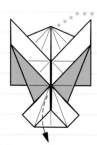

Wrap the flap around from
behind, allowing the side
corners to invert.

Wrap the side flap
around.

The fold in progress.

Wrap the right side around
in the same way.

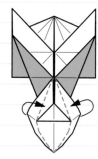

The fold in progress.

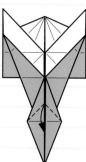

Lower the triangle
folded at step **17**.

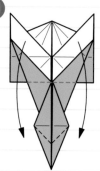

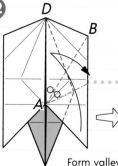

Form valley fold A-B and
squash so the resulting mountain fold lies on D-E. Refer to
page 64 for tips on folding.

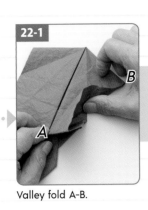
22-1

Valley fold A-B.

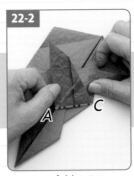
22-2

Mountain fold A-C.

22-3

Valley fold.

22-4

The structure after folding.

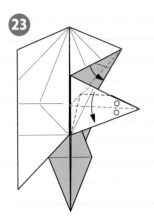
23

Swivel fold.

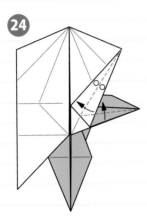
24

Swivel fold again.

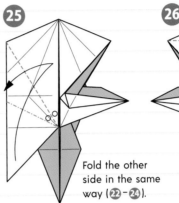
25

Fold the other side in the same way (22 – 24).

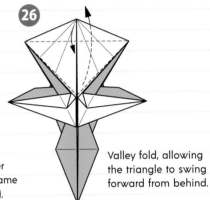
26

Valley fold, allowing the triangle to swing forward from behind.

Start applying glue on the non-visible back sides

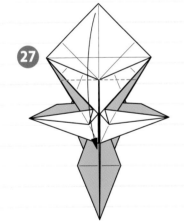
27

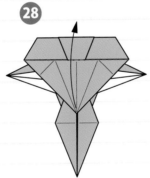
28

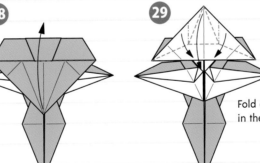
29

Fold down while swiveling in the sides.

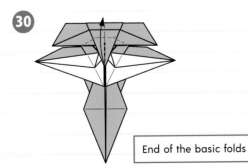
30

End of the basic folds

Valley fold up, allowing small squashes to form.

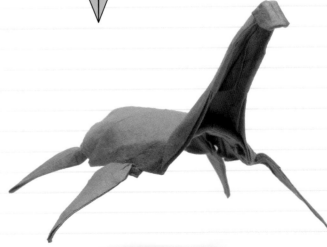

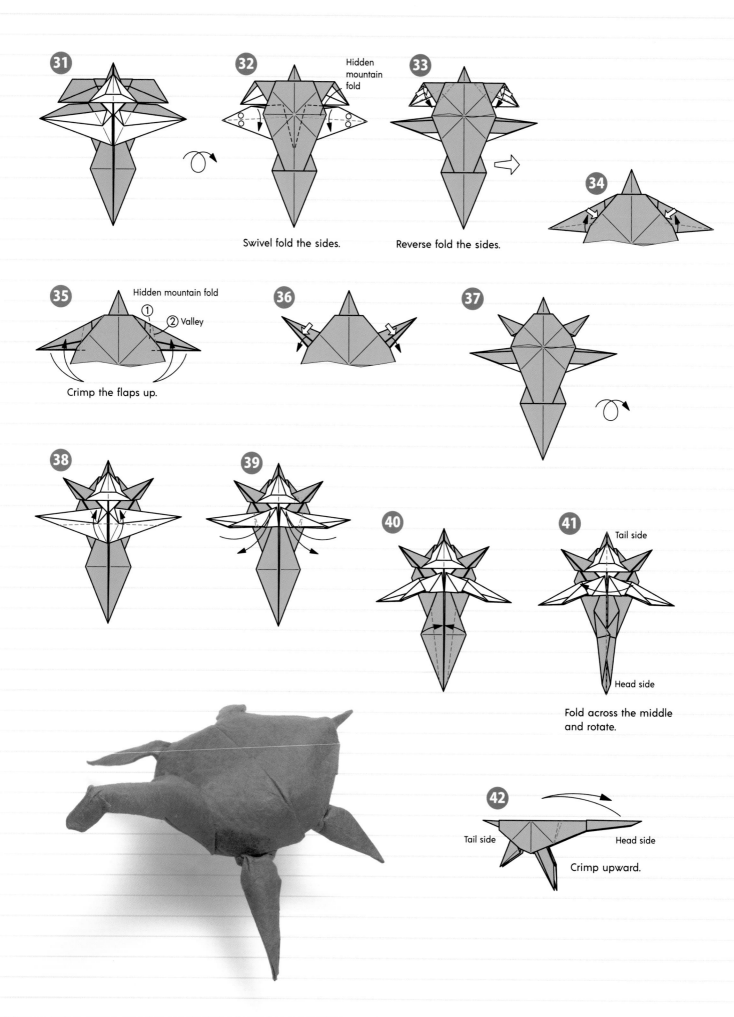

31

32 Hidden mountain fold

Swivel fold the sides.

33

Reverse fold the sides.

34

35 Hidden mountain fold
① ② Valley

Crimp the flaps up.

36

37

38

39

40

41 Tail side

Head side

Fold across the middle and rotate.

42 Tail side   Head side

Crimp upward.

68

43

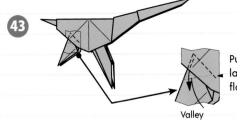

Pull out the trapped layer and squash it flat. Repeat behind.

Valley

44

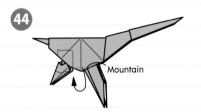

Mountain

Mountain fold the edge inside. Repeat on the other side.

45

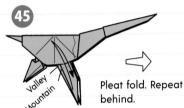

Valley
Mountain

Pleat fold. Repeat behind.

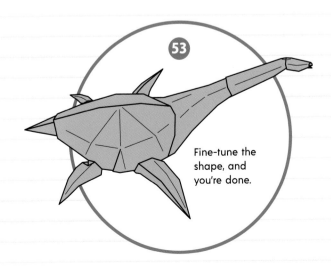

46

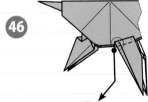

Reverse fold. Fold the three other corners in the same way.

47

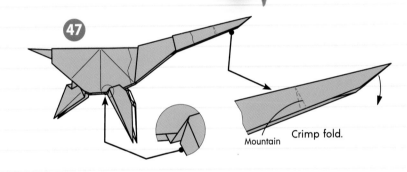

Mountain   Crimp fold.

48

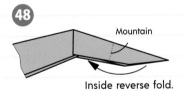

Mountain

Inside reverse fold.

49

Mountain

Tuck the corner inside. Repeat on the other side.

50

Hidden mountain fold

Reverse fold the hidden flap.

51

Mountain

Mountain fold and repeat on the other side.

52

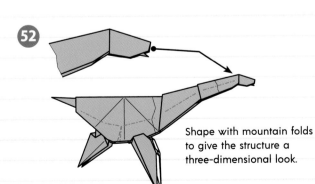

Shape with mountain folds to give the structure a three-dimensional look.

53

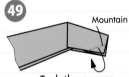

Fine-tune the shape, and you're done.

SPINOSAURUS

Type of paper used:
- Handmade Washi
- 12¼ x 12¼ inch (31 x 31 cm)
- 1 sheet

Folding Tips

For all the dinosaur movie fanatics, it might seem odd to include this dinosaur as part of an aquatic animals collection, but recent research suggest that the Spinosaurus may have spent most of its time hunting in water. To throw in another interesting fact, the Spinosaurus was bulkier than the famous Tyrannosaurus Rex, making it the largest carnivorous dinosaur of all time.

Steps 28–31 aim to recreate the sail-like structure of the dinosaur. It is indicated that glue should be applied at step 31, but the small folds between steps 19–27 can be glued in advance, as they are fragile. Steps 38–39 require a crimp fold to create the shape of the head, which can be done effectively by thinning the top of the neck with a mountain fold. This technique can be applied whenever applicable on other creations as well.

Start from the Preliminary Base (page 10)

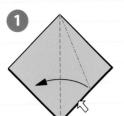

1

Open in the direction of the white arrow and squash fold.

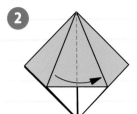

2

Swing one flap over.

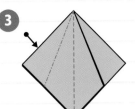

3

Repeat steps **1**–**2** on the other flap indicated by the dot-terminated arrow.

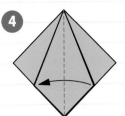

4

Swing one flap over.

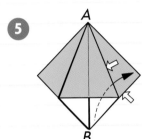

5

A

B

Open in the direction of the white arrows and squash fold. The valley A-B should become flat.

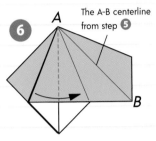

6

A

The A-B centerline from step **5**

B

Swing one flap over.

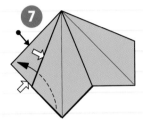

7

Repeat steps **4**–**6** on the other flap indicated by the dot-terminated arrow.

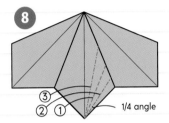

8

③
② ①

1/4 angle

Make folding lines according to the diagram.

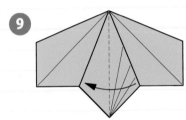

9

Swing one flap over.

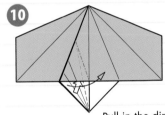

10

Pull in the direction of the white arrow and reverse fold.

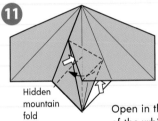

11

Hidden mountain fold

Open in the direction of the white arrows and reverse fold.

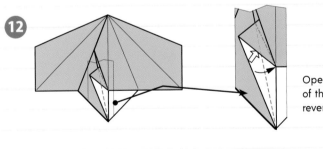

12

Open in the direction of the white arrow and reverse fold.

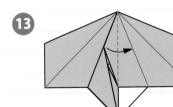

13

Swing one flap over.

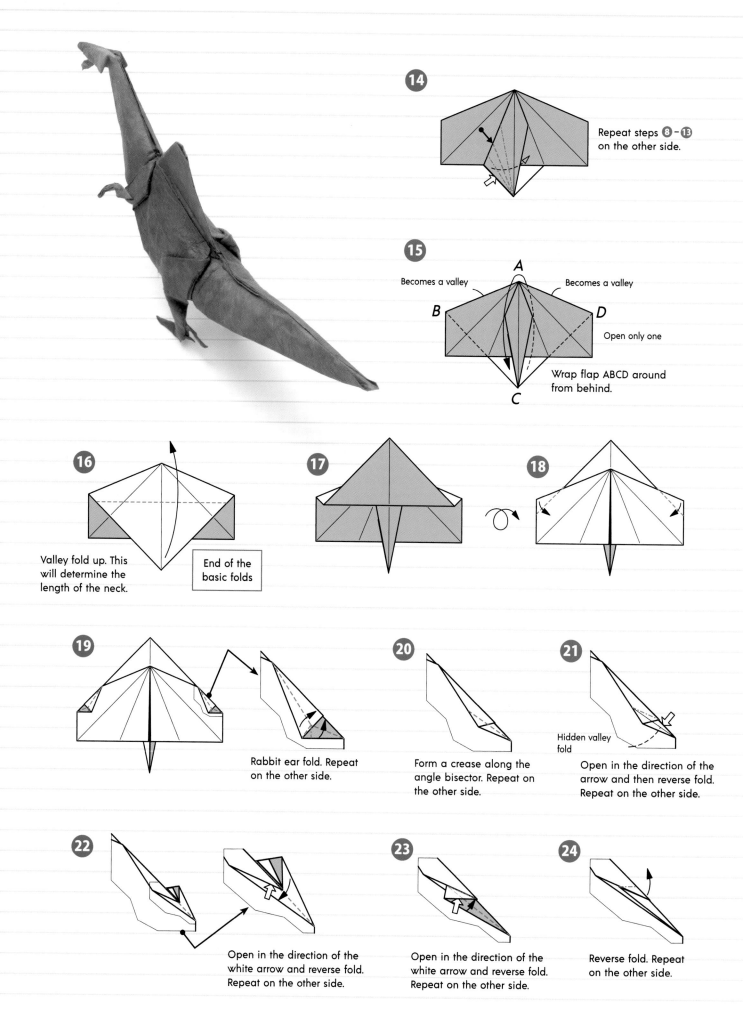

14 Repeat steps **8** – **13** on the other side.

15
A

Becomes a valley   Becomes a valley

B   D

Open only one

Wrap flap ABCD around from behind.

C

16 Valley fold up. This will determine the length of the neck.

End of the basic folds

17

18

19 Rabbit ear fold. Repeat on the other side.

20 Form a crease along the angle bisector. Repeat on the other side.

21 Hidden valley fold

Open in the direction of the arrow and then reverse fold. Repeat on the other side.

22 Open in the direction of the white arrow and reverse fold. Repeat on the other side.

23 Open in the direction of the white arrow and reverse fold. Repeat on the other side.

24 Reverse fold. Repeat on the other side.

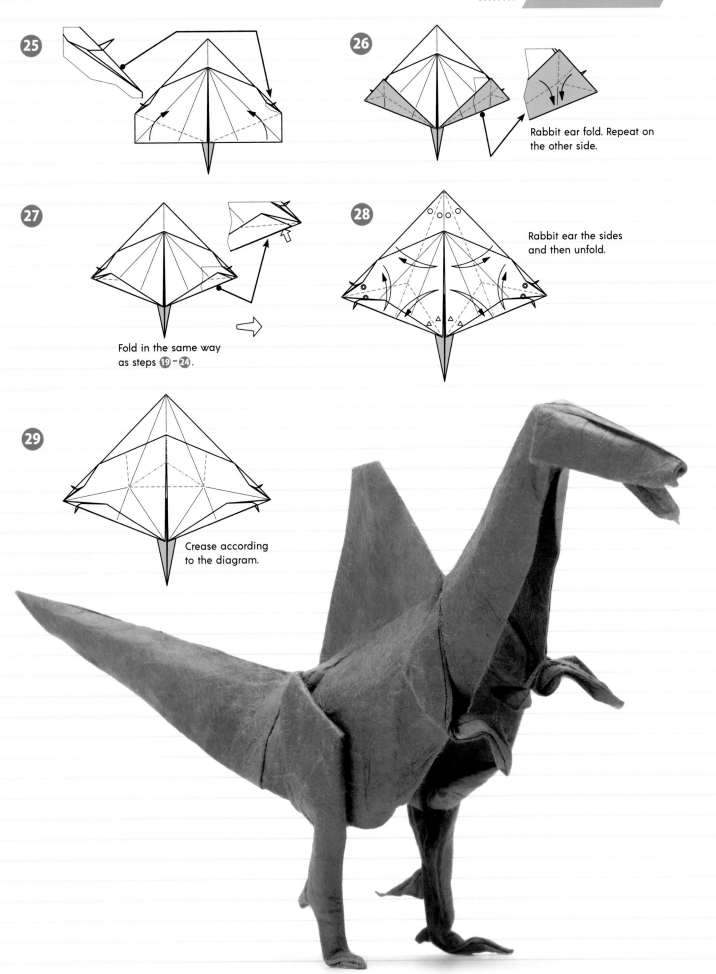

25

26 Rabbit ear fold. Repeat on the other side.

27 Fold in the same way as steps 19 – 24 .

28 Rabbit ear the sides and then unfold.

29 Crease according to the diagram.

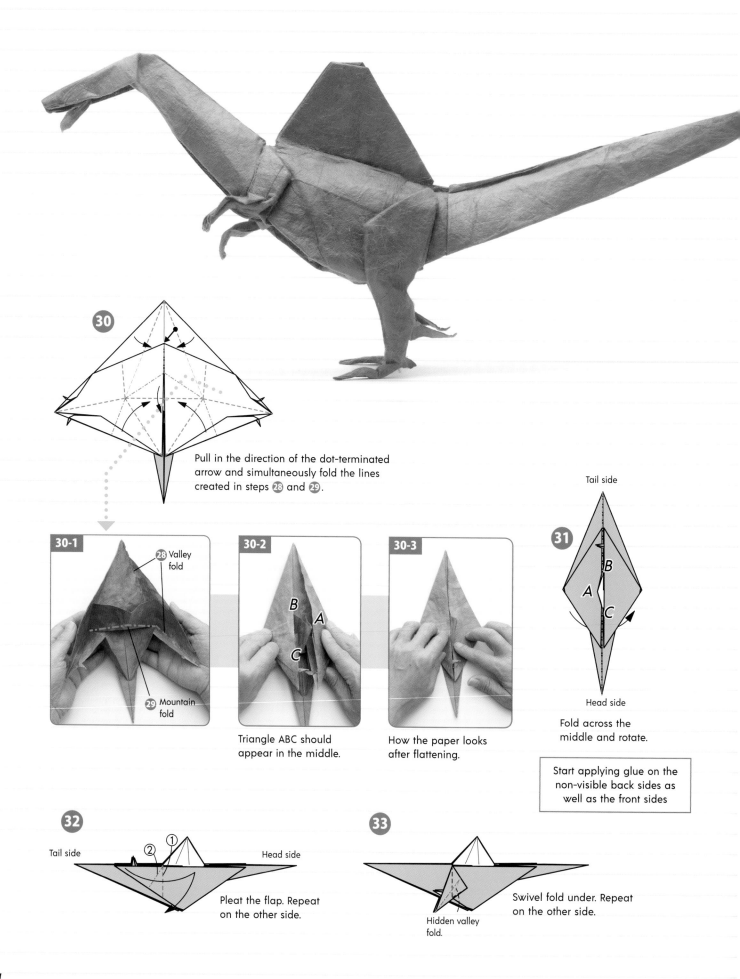

30

Pull in the direction of the dot-terminated arrow and simultaneously fold the lines created in steps **28** and **29**.

30-1
28 Valley fold
29 Mountain fold

30-2
Triangle ABC should appear in the middle.

30-3
How the paper looks after flattening.

31

Tail side

A B C

Head side

Fold across the middle and rotate.

Start applying glue on the non-visible back sides as well as the front sides

32

Tail side

② ①

Head side

Pleat the flap. Repeat on the other side.

33

Swivel fold under. Repeat on the other side.

Hidden valley fold.

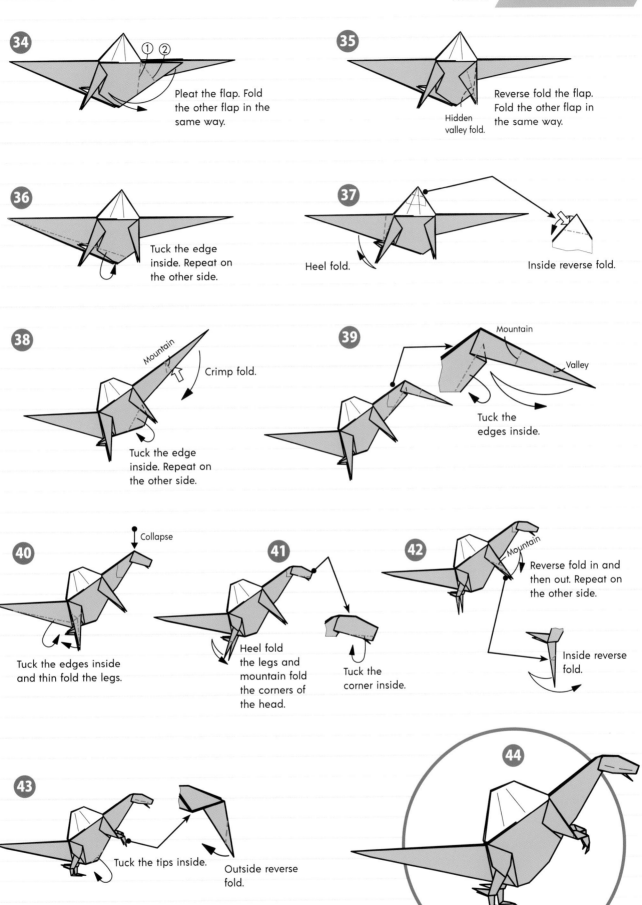

34 Pleat the flap. Fold the other flap in the same way.

35 Reverse fold the flap. Fold the other flap in the same way.

Hidden valley fold.

36 Tuck the edge inside. Repeat on the other side.

37 Heel fold.

Inside reverse fold.

38 Mountain

Crimp fold.

Tuck the edge inside. Repeat on the other side.

39 Mountain

Valley

Tuck the edges inside.

40 Collapse

Tuck the edges inside and thin fold the legs.

41 Heel fold the legs and mountain fold the corners of the head.

Tuck the corner inside.

42 Mountain

Reverse fold in and then out. Repeat on the other side.

Inside reverse fold.

43 Tuck the tips inside.

Outside reverse fold.

44 Fine-tune the shape, and you're done.

▶ Difficulty: ★★★★

ICHTHYOSAURUS

Type of paper used:
• Handmade Washi
• 12¼ x 12¼ inch (31 x 31 cm)
• 1 sheet

Folding Tips

This creation applies techniques from simpler models such as the Polar Bear (page 31) to recreate the dorsal fin cleverly using the created edge. Initially, the dorsal fin is tucked in through steps 1–9, which results in a thick layer of paper on the back side. If this becomes a problem, I recommend that you use a thinner sheet of paper for this creation. While performing step 22, do not forget to mountain fold as shown in the second image in the series of photos that illustrate the step. This fold aids in properly positioning the dorsal fin during step 22-3. You can apply glue as early as after step 7, when the petal fold has been completed. Apply glue to the non-visible back sides as usual. When finalizing, I recommend that you add volume to the body by using soft mountain folds. In the same way as folding the Swordfish (page 46), you can add realism to the head by thinning through mountain folding. Furthermore, pinching the top of the head and then slightly pulling backward will result in a nicely formed forehead and eyes.

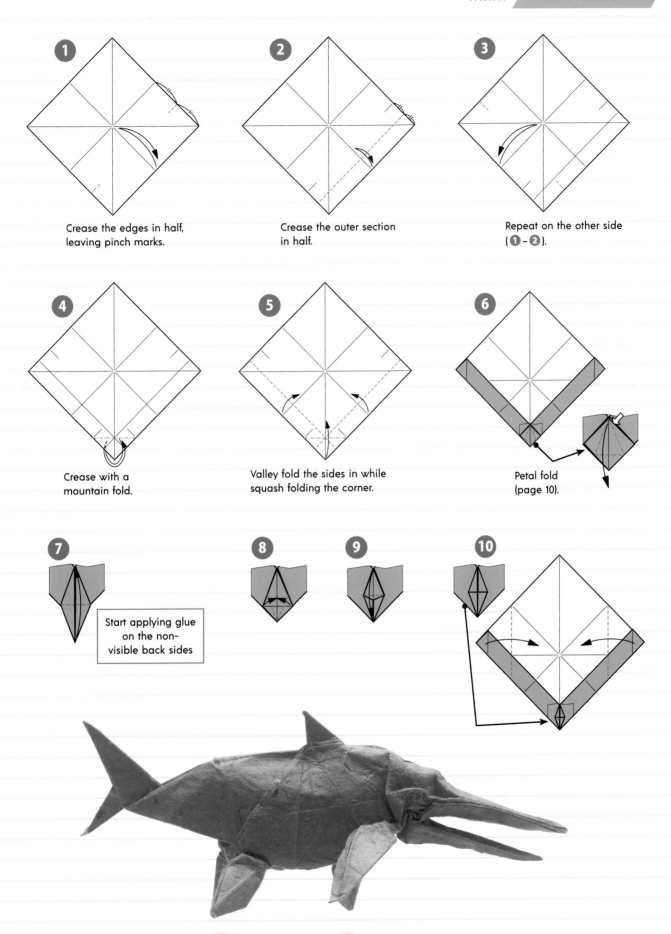

1 Crease the edges in half, leaving pinch marks.

2 Crease the outer section in half.

3 Repeat on the other side (**1**–**2**).

4 Crease with a mountain fold.

5 Valley fold the sides in while squash folding the corner.

6 Petal fold (page 10).

7 Start applying glue on the non-visible back sides

8

9

10

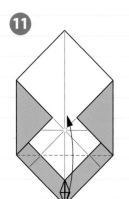
11

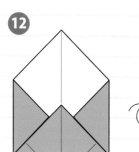
12

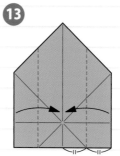
13

Valley fold to the center, allowing the flaps from behind to flip forward.

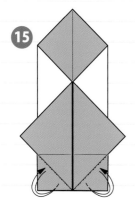
14

Crease the upper layer.

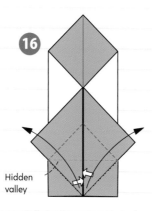
15

Crease with mountain folds.

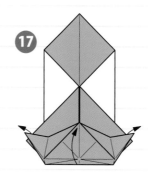
16

Hidden valley

Pull the corners outward, squashing the sides flat, and allowing the flap from behind to swing forward.

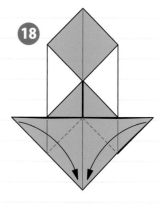
17

Step **16** in progress.

18

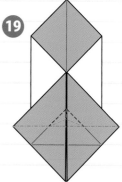
19

Crease with a mountain fold. Then rabbit ear fold the triangle on the inside.

Head side

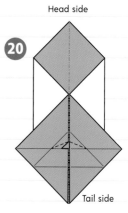
20

Tail side

Fold across the middle and rotate.

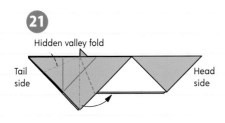

21

Hidden valley fold

Tail side ... Head side

Pull the corner over and squash fold flat.

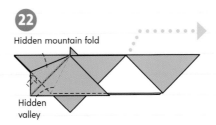

22

Hidden mountain fold

Hidden valley

Reverse fold the edge inside.

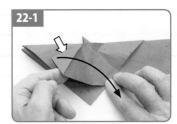

22-1

Open up in the direction of the white arrow.

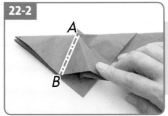

22-2

A
B

Mountain fold A-B.

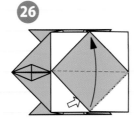

22-3

Valley fold back over.

22-4

Image of the structure after the fold.

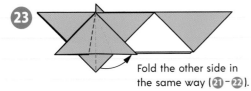

23 Fold the other side in the same way (21–22).

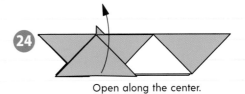

24 Open along the center.

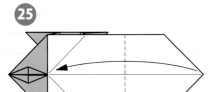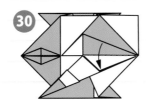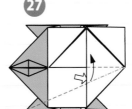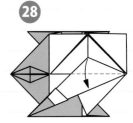

25

26

27

28

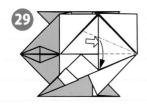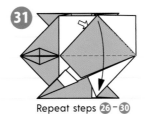

29

30

31 Repeat steps 26–30 on the other side.

32 Petal fold (page 11).

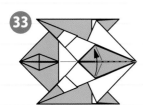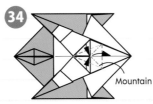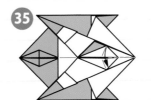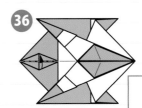

33 Swing up two flaps.

34 Petal fold.

Mountain

35 Swing the two flaps back down. Repeat steps 33–35 on the other side.

36

End of the basic folds

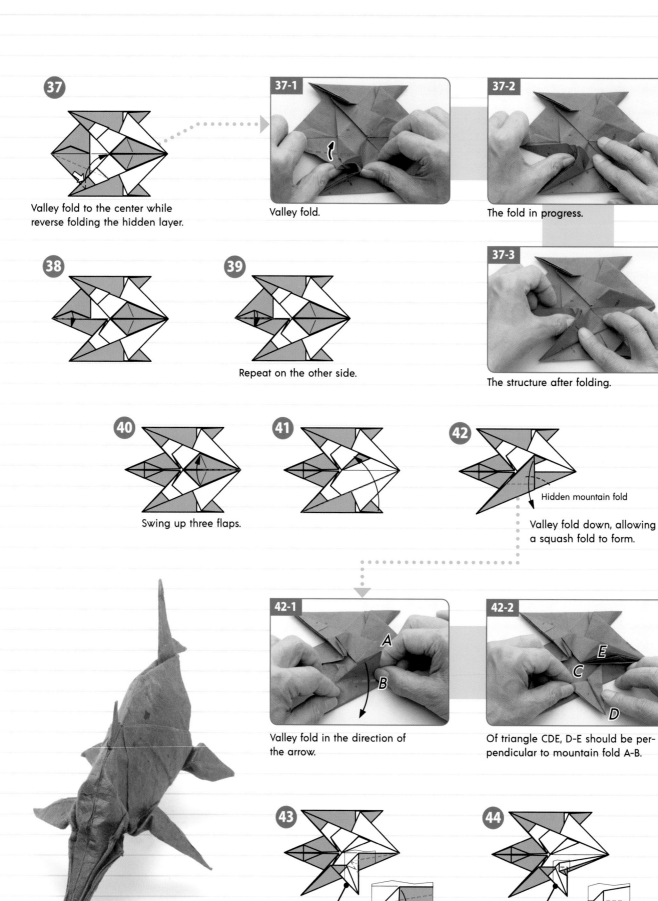

37

Valley fold to the center while reverse folding the hidden layer.

37-1

Valley fold.

37-2

The fold in progress.

37-3

The structure after folding.

38

39

Repeat on the other side.

40

Swing up three flaps.

41

42

Hidden mountain fold

Valley fold down, allowing a squash fold to form.

42-1

A

B

Valley fold in the direction of the arrow.

42-2

E

C

D

Of triangle CDE, D-E should be perpendicular to mountain fold A-B.

43

Mountain

Swivel fold.

44

Reverse fold.

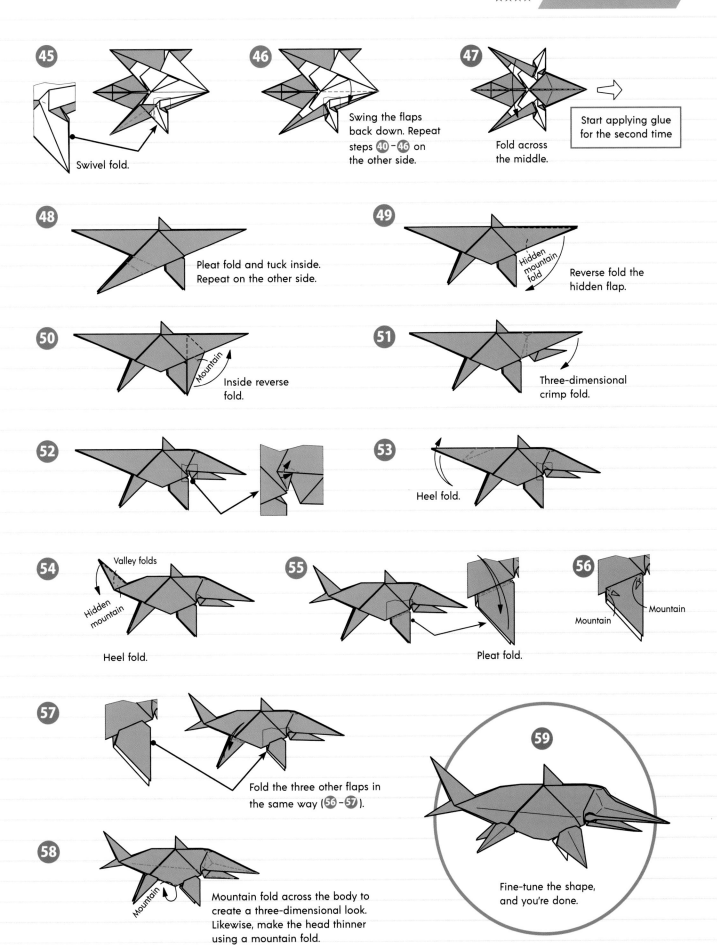

45 Swivel fold.

46 Swing the flaps back down. Repeat steps **40**–**46** on the other side.

47 Fold across the middle.

Start applying glue for the second time

48 Pleat fold and tuck inside. Repeat on the other side.

49 Hidden mountain fold Reverse fold the hidden flap.

50 Mountain Inside reverse fold.

51 Three-dimensional crimp fold.

52

53 Heel fold.

54 Valley folds Hidden mountain Heel fold.

55 Pleat fold.

56 Mountain Mountain

57 Fold the three other flaps in the same way (**56**–**57**).

58 Mountain Mountain fold across the body to create a three-dimensional look. Likewise, make the head thinner using a mountain fold.

59 Fine-tune the shape, and you're done.

CRAB

Type of paper used:
- Washi
- 15¾ x 15¾ inch (40 x 40 cm)
- 1 sheet

Folding Tips

The essential procedure for this model is quite similar to that for the Cicada or the Japanese Horned Beetle featured in *Fantastic Origami Flying Creatures*, but I published this book first, so I've dubbed this the "Crab Fold." The procedure is lengthy, but it mainly consists of a repetition of the same steps. I call for applying glue on the inside surfaces after step 10, followed by another round of gluing after step 38. The particular type of sheet used for this creation is a little tough to glue together, so pay attention when going through the process. When executing step 38, fold as close to the body as possible to make the legs look longer. During step 47, a deep mountain fold will result in a more realistic shape, as crabs are generally not very long. Lastly, make sure that the bases of the claws do not end up being thicker than the claws themselves. There's a lot going on with this model, but you'll get through it if you focus and follow the steps carefully until the end.

1

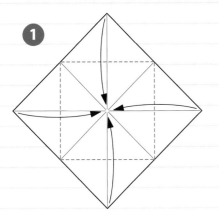

2

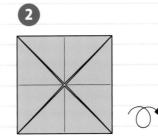

3

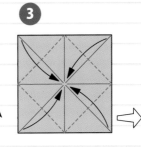

4

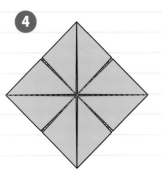

Fold a Preliminary
Base (page 10).

5

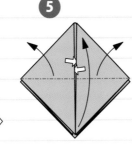

Open out the sides and
squash fold.

6

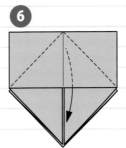

Pull out the flap from
the inside.

7

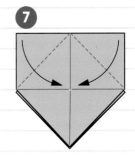

8

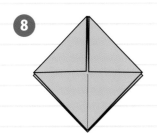

Fold the three other sides in
the same way (**5**-**7**).

9

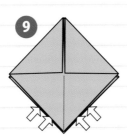

Open out the Prelimi-
nary Base formation.

10

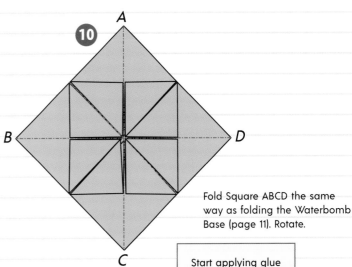

Fold Square ABCD the same
way as folding the Waterbomb
Base (page 11). Rotate.

Start applying glue
on the inside portions

11

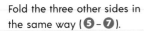

Petal fold (page 10).
Fold the three other
sides in the same way.

12

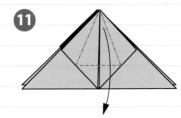

Open out the Waterbomb Base
and fold it back into a Preliminary
Base formation.

13

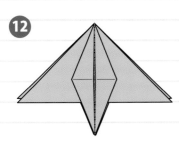

14

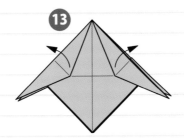

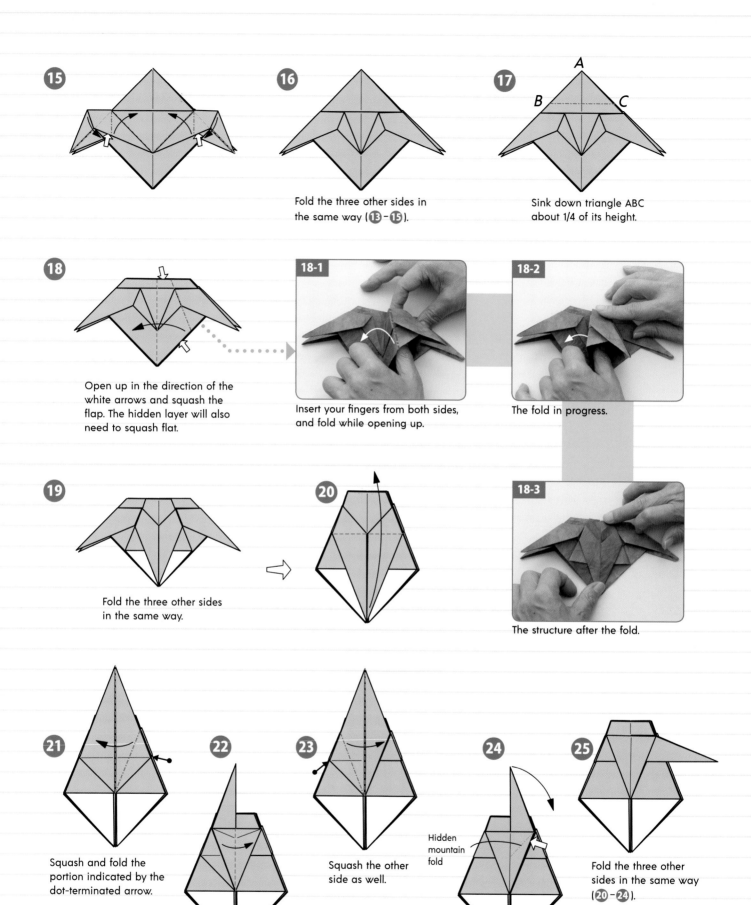

15

16 Fold the three other sides in the same way (**13**–**15**).

17 Sink down triangle ABC about 1/4 of its height.

A
B   C

18 Open up in the direction of the white arrows and squash the flap. The hidden layer will also need to squash flat.

18-1 Insert your fingers from both sides, and fold while opening up.

18-2 The fold in progress.

18-3 The structure after the fold.

19 Fold the three other sides in the same way.

20

21 Squash and fold the portion indicated by the dot-terminated arrow.

22 Swing a flap over.

23 Squash the other side as well.

24 Hidden mountain fold

25 Fold the three other sides in the same way (**20**–**24**).

26

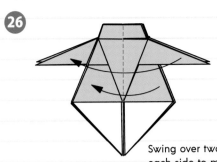

Swing over two flaps at each side to make the model symmetrical.

27

Hidden valley fold.

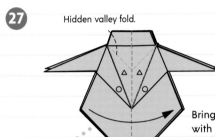

Bring together the two triangles with a valley fold and pinch the two circles so as to draw them out in front.

27-1

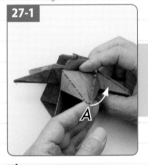

Lift corner A to create two mountain folds.

27-2

Valley fold down the center.

27-3

Pinch and fold toward each other.

27-4

Fold and tilt toward the right.

28

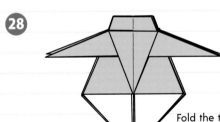

Fold the three other sides in the same way (**26** – **27**).

29

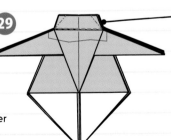

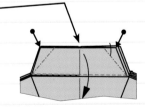

Squash in the direction indicated by the dot-terminated arrows and fold.

30

Tuck the indicated part inside.

31

Fold the three other sides in the same way (**29** – **30**).

32

Reverse fold for all four flaps.

33

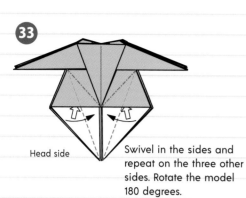

Head side

Swivel in the sides and repeat on the three other sides. Rotate the model 180 degrees.

34

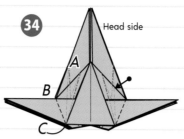

Head side

A

B

C

Sink triangle ABC. Do the same with the other side.

End of the basic folds

35

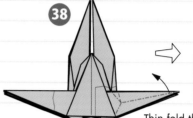

Turn over.

36

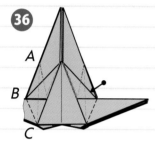

A

B

C

Sink triangle ABC. Do the same with the other side.

37

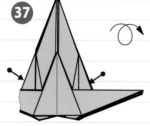

Repeat step **36** on the inner flaps. Turn over.

38

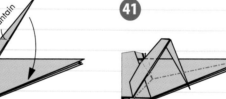

Apply glue for the second time

Thin fold the flap.

39

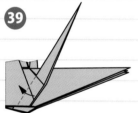

Valley fold both sides of the flap over.

40

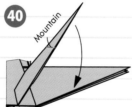

Mountain

Inside reverse fold.

41

Fold all the other legs in the same way (**38**–**40**).

42

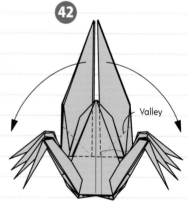

Valley

Outside reverse fold the four flaps.

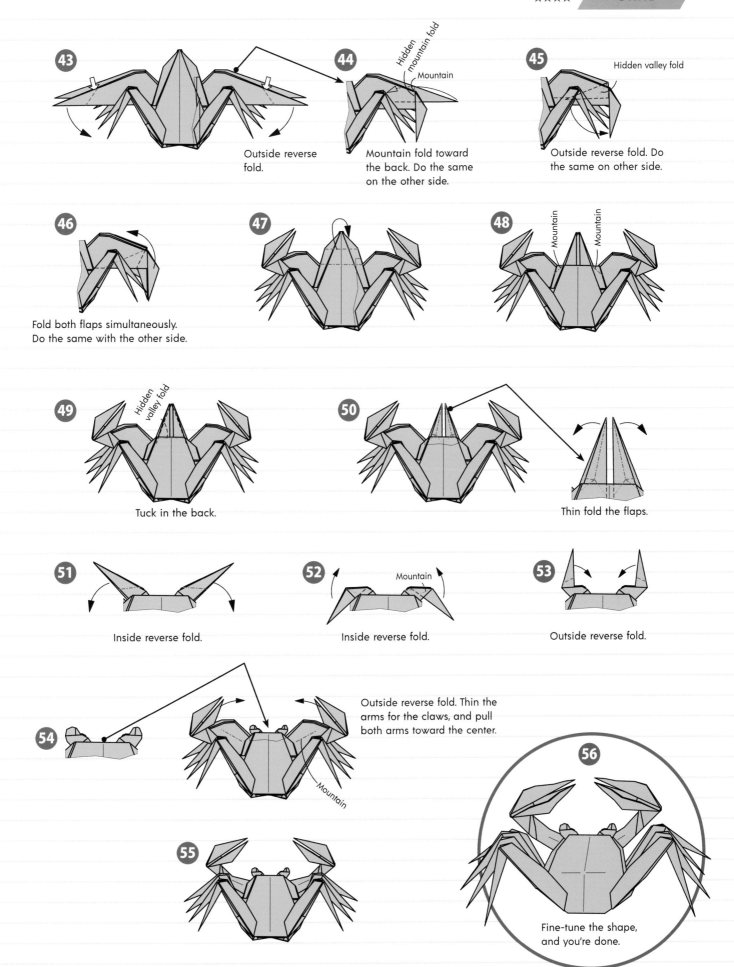

43 Outside reverse fold.

44 Hidden mountain fold / Mountain — Mountain fold toward the back. Do the same on the other side.

45 Hidden valley fold — Outside reverse fold. Do the same on other side.

46 Fold both flaps simultaneously. Do the same with the other side.

47

48 Mountain   Mountain

49 Hidden valley fold — Tuck in the back.

50 Thin fold the flaps.

51 Inside reverse fold.

52 Mountain — Inside reverse fold.

53 Outside reverse fold.

54 Outside reverse fold. Thin the arms for the claws, and pull both arms toward the center. Mountain

55

56 Fine-tune the shape, and you're done.

MARINE ISOPOD

Type of paper used:
- Handmade Washi (momigami)
- 12¼ x 12¼ inch (31 x 31 cm)
- 1 sheet

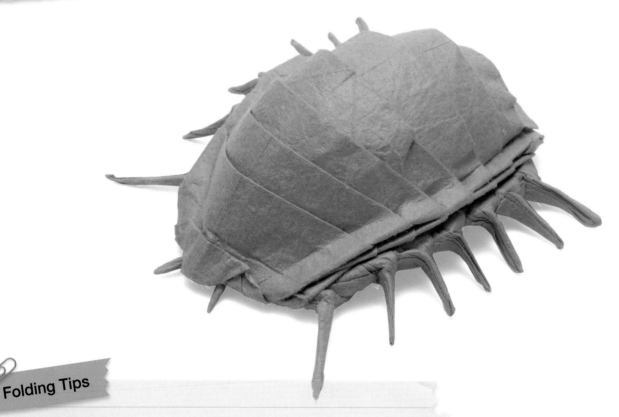

Folding Tips

To make the model in the photograph above, I used a relatively coarse type of paper called "momigami," which is a durable material that doesn't have the tendency to rip at the corners during folding. If you seek this type of paper out, it might take some time to find a suitable sheet, as wrinkles and uneven sides are common. As a last resort, you can soak a wrinkled sheet of momigami paper in water and spread the wrinkles flat while it dries to prepare it for folding.

This model does not start with a base, but up until step 30 it should be fairly simple to follow the diagrams faithfully. Step 31 involves pulling the antennae and the legs toward the head, balancing the overall shape. This is also the point at which the lengths of the legs can be adjusted. Apply glue during this step. However, during step 40, we will further shape the segments of the back, so avoid spreading glue on these parts as well as on the stomach.

1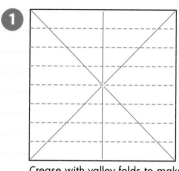

Crease with valley folds to make eight equal segments.

2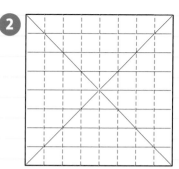

Crease vertically in the same way. Turn over.

3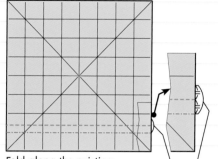

Fold along the existing mountain fold and pleat upward at about 1/3rd the height of the division above.

About 3/4 of 1/8 of the side of the sheet

4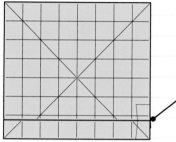

Repeat the pleating process six more times using the existing mountain fold lines.

This indicated width is 1/3rd the height of the original 1/8th division below.

5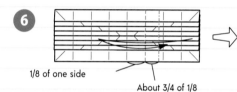

6

1/8 of one side

About 3/4 of 1/8

Valley fold along the existing 1/8 crease and pleat back leaving about a 1/3rd gap from the center.

7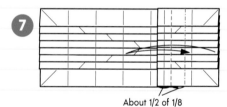

About 1/2 of 1/8

Pleat fold. Place the mountain fold first at 1/2 the width from the original center crease. The valley fold falls at the halfway point between the two folded edges.

8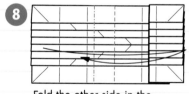

Fold the other side in the same way (**6** – **7**).

9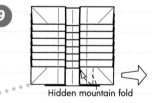

Hidden mountain fold

Reverse fold the hidden corner.

9-1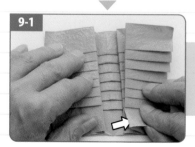

Open up in the direction of the white arrow.

9-2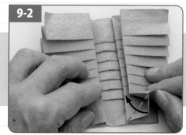

Reverse fold.

9-3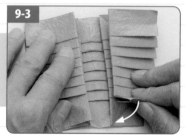

Close.

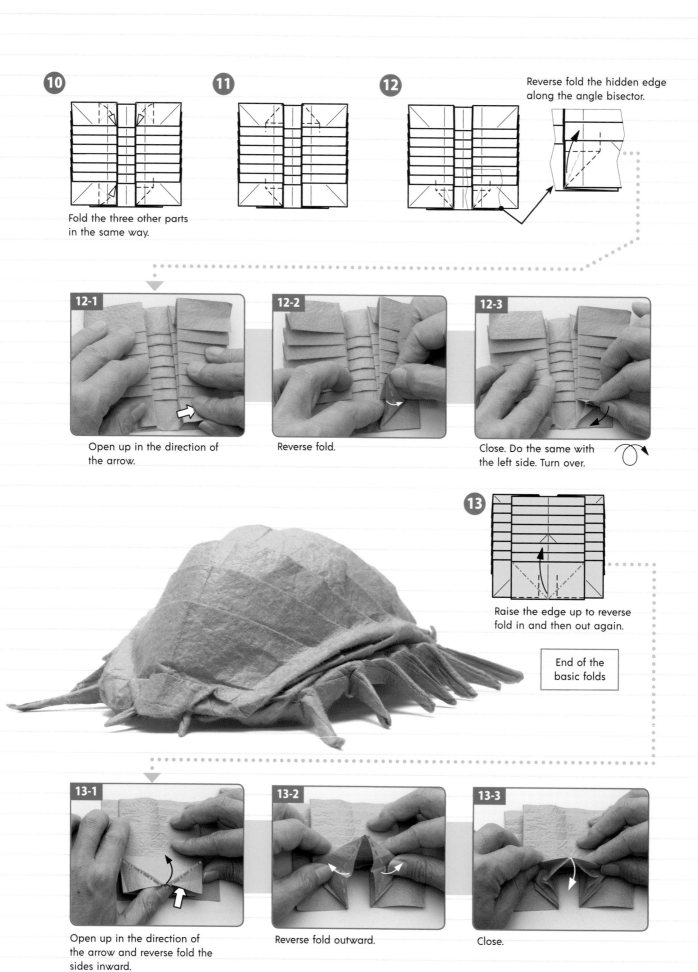

10

Fold the three other parts in the same way.

11

12

Reverse fold the hidden edge along the angle bisector.

12-1

Open up in the direction of the arrow.

12-2

Reverse fold.

12-3

Close. Do the same with the left side. Turn over.

13

Raise the edge up to reverse fold in and then out again.

End of the basic folds

13-1

Open up in the direction of the arrow and reverse fold the sides inward.

13-2

Reverse fold outward.

13-3

Close.

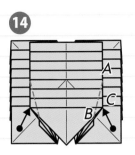

14

Sink triangle ABC. Repeat on the other side.

15

Inside reverse fold both sides.

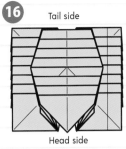

16

Tail side

Head side

Turn over and rotate.

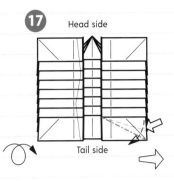

17

Head side

Tail side

18

Hidden mountain fold

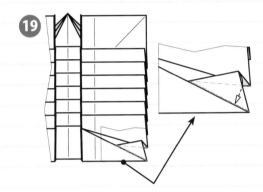

19

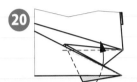

20

21

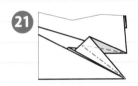

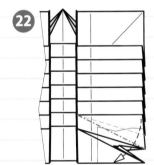

22

Fold the remaining pleats on both sides in the same way (**17**–**21**).

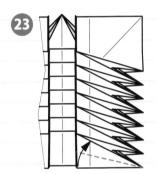

23

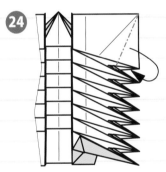

24

91

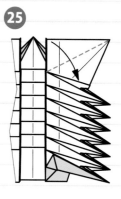
25

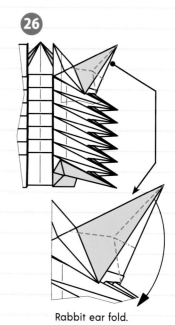
26

Rabbit ear fold.

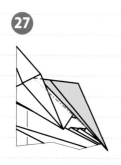
27

28

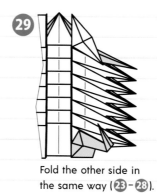
29

Fold the other side in
the same way (**23**–**28**).

Corner

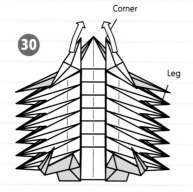
30

Leg

Pull up the two corners (with
the seven legs) so they extend
beyond the top point.

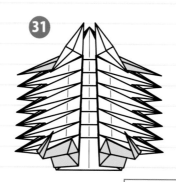
31

Apply glue except for on
the back and stomach, as
explained in the introduction

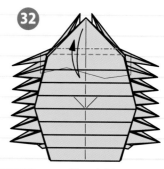
32

Pleat fold.

33

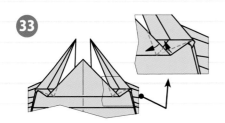

34

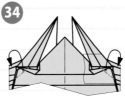

Tuck in.

35

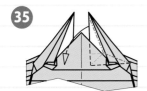

Thin fold the flap.

36

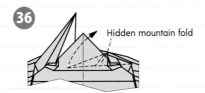

Hidden mountain fold

37

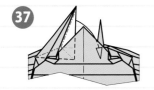

Fold the other side in the same way (**36**–**35**).

38

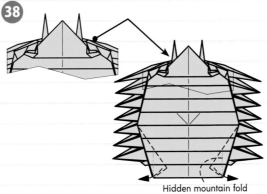

Hidden mountain fold

Reverse fold.

39

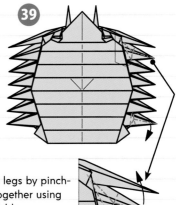

Thin all the legs by pinching them together using mountain folds.

40

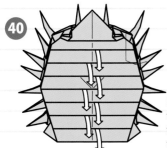

Pull out the segments on the back and shape them to make the body look three dimensional.

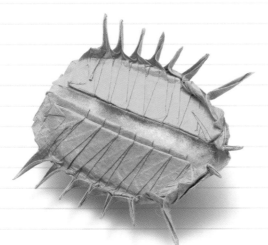

Optionally, stuff cotton or tissue into the cavity for a more solid shape.

41

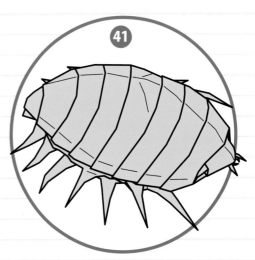

Fine-tune the shape, and you're done.

SQUID

Type of paper used:
- Washi
- 12¼ x 12¼ inch (31 x 31 cm)
- 1 sheet

Folding Tips

The 8-division pleat fold is applied to this creation to generate 5 corners on each side, allowing for 10 corners in total. Modifying the corners into tentacles facilitates the creation of a squid, which is where the original idea came from. The tentacles are folded in the same way as the Crocodile's claws (page 58), but we added another step here (step 14, to be specific), to create very thin structures. You should apply the glue after step 20 when the squashing maneuvers of steps 16 and 18 are complete, but make sure not to spread glue onto the back part hanging between the tentacles. Step 37 is performed to make the tentacles appear longer, by simultaneously valley folding 5 at a time. The final step should include the gluing of each of the 10 tentacles, allowing the structure to stand on its own.

1

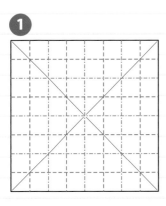

Crease the paper by pleating into eighths in both directions. Turn over.

2

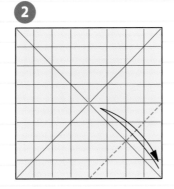

Crease the corner.

3

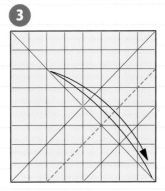

Crease again.

4

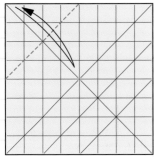

Fold the other three corners in the same way (**2** - **3**).

5

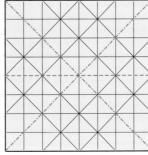

Fold into a Waterbomb Base (page 11).

6

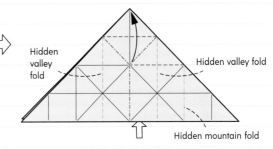

Hidden valley fold

Hidden valley fold

Hidden mountain fold

Pinch the top layer in half along its center, allowing its sides to squash fold flat. Swing the resulting flap over to the right.

7

Open up in the direction of the white arrow and squash fold.

8

9

Fold the back side in the same way (**6** - **8**).

10

Open up in the direction of the arrow and inside reverse fold.

11

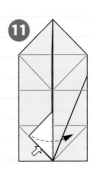

Open up in the direction of the white arrow and inside reverse fold.

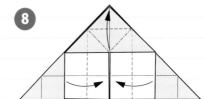

OCTOPUS

Type of paper used:
- Handmade Washi
- 12¼ x 12¼ inch (31 x 31 cm)
- 1 sheet

Folding Tips

The series of photos that describe step 4 show the paper opened out to be rearranged, but it differs to the Wrap and Reform Layers maneuver introduced at the bottom of page 9. During step 9, you'll perform a squashing procedure, and two triangles should form as seen in step 10. Steps 10–12 are rather challenging, but at step 14, eight tentacles will be formed. Begin to apply glue at this stage. Refer to page 12 to for details about applying glue and then returning your model to its original shape. Step 16 is where the model really comes to life. Apply glue to the inner sides of the tentacles to give them lively, curving shapes. In addition, tilting the head downward and shaping some of the folds into eyes will add pleasing realism to your finished model.

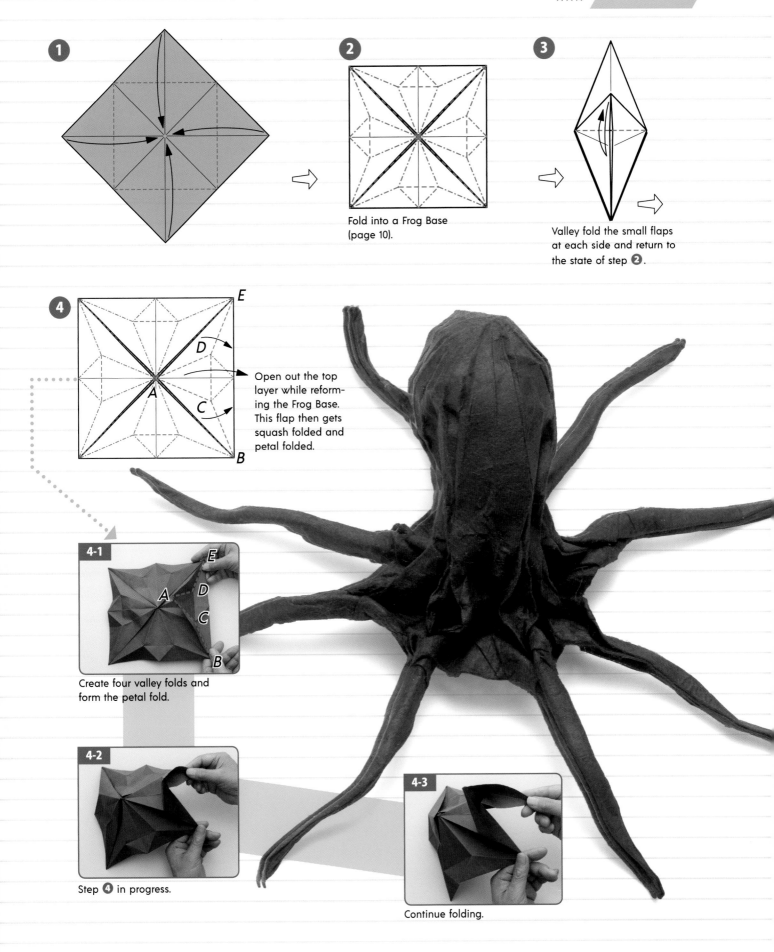

1

2

Fold into a Frog Base
(page 10).

3

Valley fold the small flaps
at each side and return to
the state of step **2**.

4

E

D

A

C

B

Open out the top
layer while reform-
ing the Frog Base.
This flap then gets
squash folded and
petal folded.

4-1

E

A

D

C

B

Create four valley folds and
form the petal fold.

4-2

Step **4** in progress.

4-3

Continue folding.

5

Step **4** in progress.

6

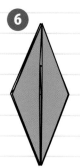

Fold the three other sides in the same way.

7

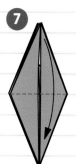

Fold the three other sides in the same way.

8

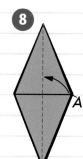

Lift corner A up vertically.

9

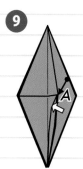

Squash fold corner A and the raised flap above in the direction indicated by the dot-terminated arrow.

10

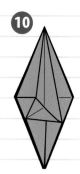

Fold the seven other sides in the same way, and arrange them symmetrically.

11

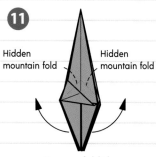

Hidden mountain fold   Hidden mountain fold

Reverse fold the eight tentacles.

12

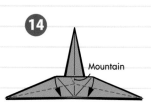

13

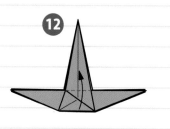

Fold the other sides in the same way.

14

Mountain

End of the basic folds

Start applying glue on the back sides of the tentacles

15

Fold the other sides in the same way.

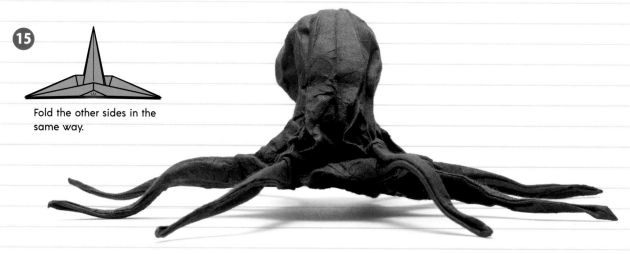

16

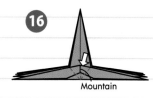

Mountain

Open up in the direction of the white arrow to give the structure a three-dimensional shape.

17

Add volume to the body by blowing air into it like you would with a balloon.

18

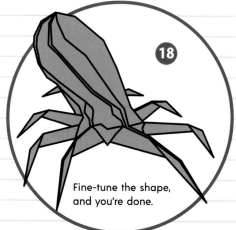

Fine-tune the shape, and you're done.

GIANT SQUID

▶ Difficulty: ★★★

Type of paper used:
- Handmade Washi
- 15¾ x 15¾ inch (40 x 40 cm)
- 1 sheet

Folding Tips

Giant Squid are a popular subject of fascination, and like their tentacles, there are a few things we have to keep an eye on when folding this model. First of all, the basic folds method is entirely different from the "ordinary" Squid (page 94).

The two long tentacles are folded at the beginning, followed by the smaller ones. If you find it difficult to maneuver around the long tentacles, fold them back until the end. The outside reverse fold in step 25 is challenging to perform, and so I recommend that you angle the long tentacles outward to facilitate folding. Start applying glue at step 37, this time on both sides, only omitting the areas where folding is necessary to give the tentacles their shape. Spreading the tips of the long tentacles gives them a more realistic look, so avoid spreading glue on these parts as well. To finish, orient the small tentacles in such a way that all eight of them are visible when the model is viewed from the front.

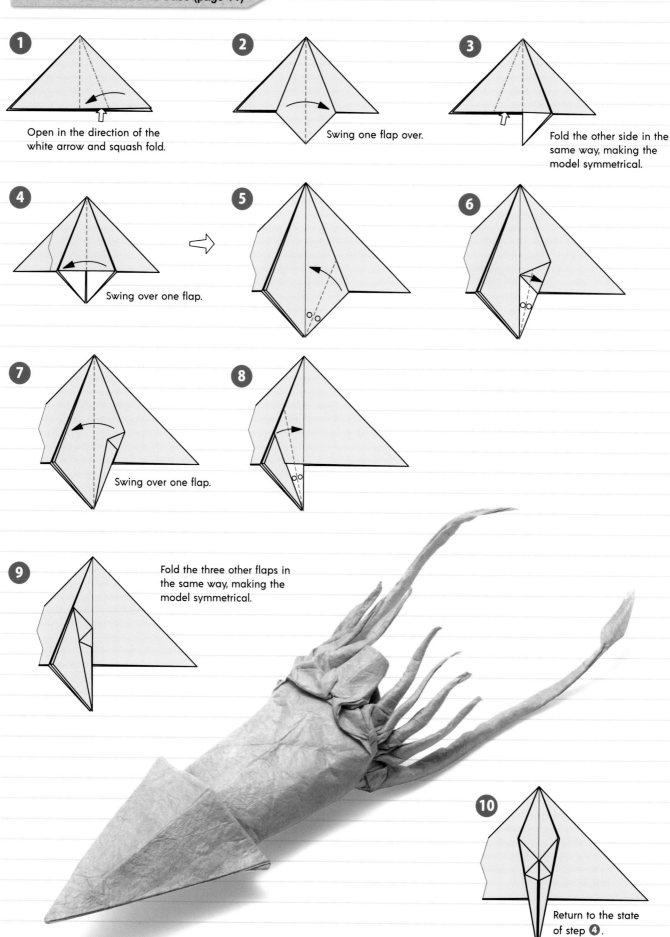

1 Open in the direction of the white arrow and squash fold.

2 Swing one flap over.

3 Fold the other side in the same way, making the model symmetrical.

4 Swing over one flap.

5

6

7 Swing over one flap.

8

9 Fold the three other flaps in the same way, making the model symmetrical.

10 Return to the state of step **4**.

11

Swing over
two flaps.

12

Open up in the direction of the white arrow and reverse fold.

13

Crease along the center.

14

Open up in the direction of the white arrow and reverse fold.

15

Open up in the direction of the white arrow and squash fold.

16

Fold the three other flaps in the same way, making the model symmetrical.

17

Return to the state of step ❶ to make it simpler to fold the two long tentacles.

18

19

Crease, using mountain and valley folds along the indicated divisions.

20

Open up in the direction of the white arrow and squash fold.

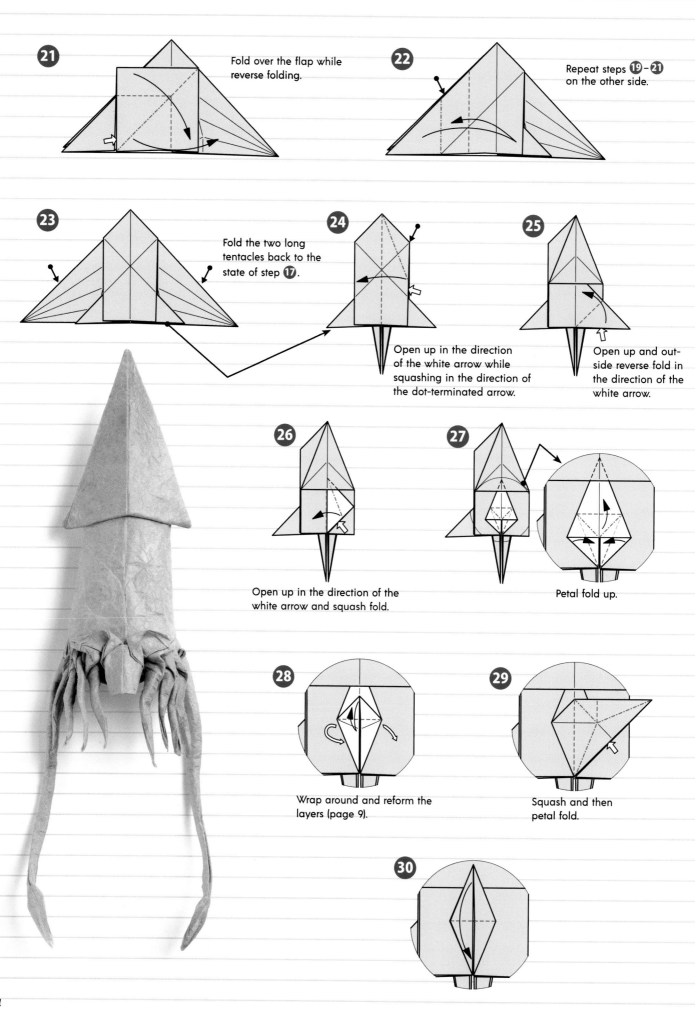

21 Fold over the flap while reverse folding.

22 Repeat steps **19**–**21** on the other side.

23 Fold the two long tentacles back to the state of step **17**.

24 Open up in the direction of the white arrow while squashing in the direction of the dot-terminated arrow.

25 Open up and outside reverse fold in the direction of the white arrow.

26 Open up in the direction of the white arrow and squash fold.

27 Petal fold up.

28 Wrap around and reform the layers (page 9).

29 Squash and then petal fold.

30

31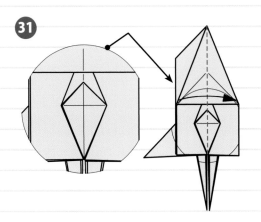

32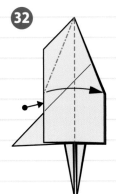

Repeat steps **24**–**31** on the other side.

33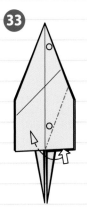

Open up in the direction of the white arrow and inside reverse fold.

34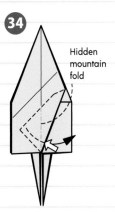

Hidden mountain fold

Open up in the direction of the white arrow and reverse fold.

35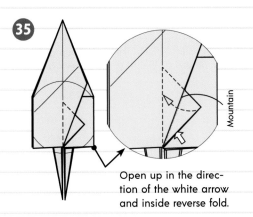

Open up in the direction of the white arrow and inside reverse fold.

36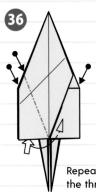

Repeat steps **33**–**35** on the three other flaps.

37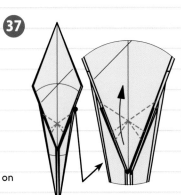

End of the basic folds

Start applying glue on all the back sides except the two long tentacles

Rabbit ear the flap, and then squash fold it. Tiny squash folds will form at the edges.

38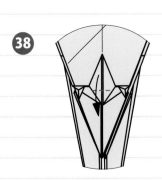

39

Mountain

Tuck inside.

40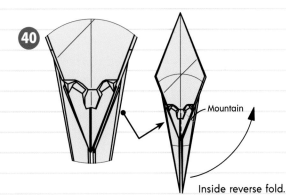

Mountain

Inside reverse fold.

41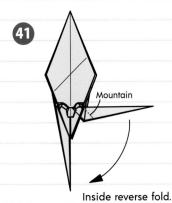

Mountain

Inside reverse fold.

42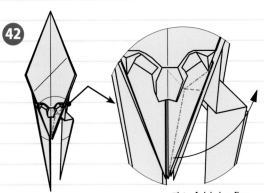

Thin fold the flap.

43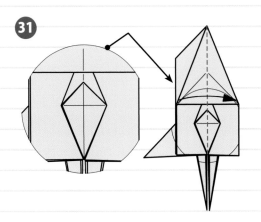

Mountain

Inside reverse fold.

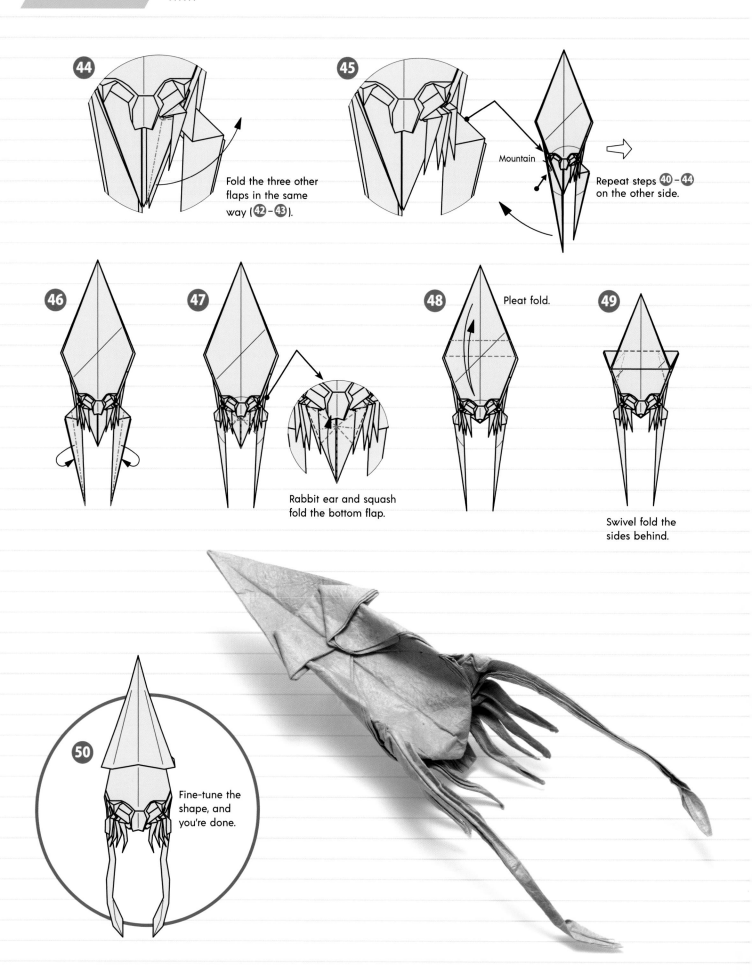

44 Fold the three other flaps in the same way (**42**–**43**).

45 Mountain. Repeat steps **40**–**44** on the other side.

46

47 Rabbit ear and squash fold the bottom flap.

48 Pleat fold.

49 Swivel fold the sides behind.

50 Fine-tune the shape, and you're done.

JELLYFISH

Type of paper used:
• Handmade Washi
• 15¾ x 15¾ inch (40 x 40 cm)
• 1 sheet

Folding Tips

As with my Praying Mantis model (featured in another one of my books), this model has eight Bird Bases that come together from a single sheet of paper. At step 36, twelve long tentacles and eight short tentacles will have been formed, all from corners of the individual Bird Bases. Begin applying glue to the back sides of the tentacles at step 36. As you fold steps 36–42, the model will become a three-dimensional shape. Refer to the series of photos to achieve a realistic appearance. To add volume to the body, cotton or tissue can be inserted from the underside of the bell. Doing so makes the structure much more stable. If possible, fold the smaller tentacles to make them thinner, which adds to the realism.

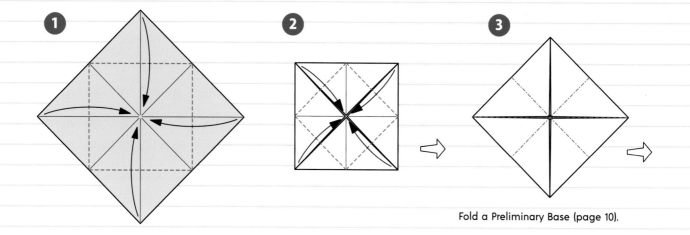

Fold a Preliminary Base (page 10).

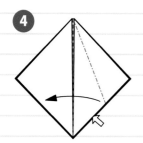

4 Open up in the direction of the white arrow and squash fold.

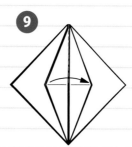

5 Petal fold (page 10).

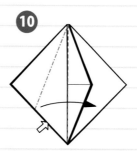

6 Wrap around and reform (page 9).

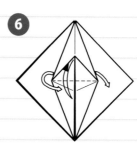

7 Open up in the direction of the white arrow and squash fold.

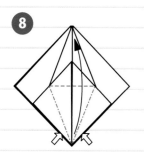

8 Petal fold.

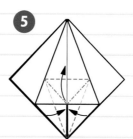

9 Swing over two flaps.

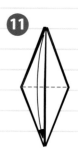

10 Fold the other three flaps in the same way (4 - 8).

11

12 Open up one flap.

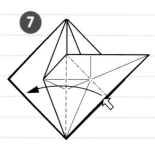

13 Lift while opening up the bottom side.

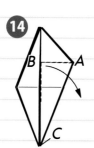

14 Pull out triangle ABC from the inside.

15 Swing over three flaps.

16

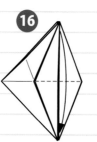

17 Repeat steps 12 - 14.

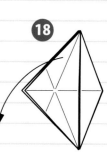

18 Pull out the trapped corner.

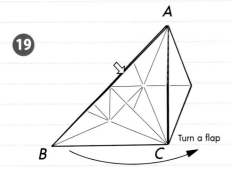

19 Wrap around triangle ABC. You will have to open the model slightly to accomplish this.

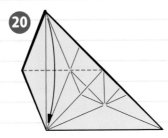

20 Valley fold. Repeat on the other side.

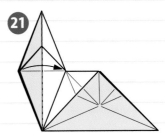

21 Swing over two flaps.

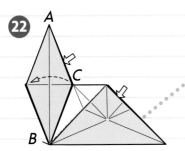

22 Squash fold triangle ABC behind, shifting the hidden flaps until the model becomes symmetrical.

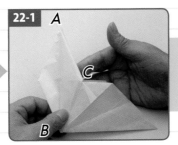

22-1 Insert a finger and keep checking until all the sides have the same thickness.

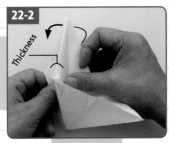

22-2 Thickness

The turning in progress.

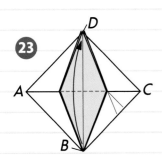

23 Only fold the overlapping triangle ABC. Make sure to place corner B onto corner D.

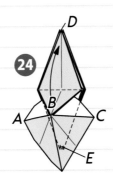

24 Step **23** in progress. Place corner B onto corner D. E should still point downward.

22-3 The structure after turning.

25 Swing over one flap.

26

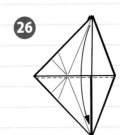

27 Swing over one flap.

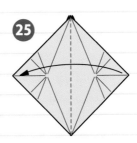

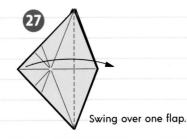

22-4 Turning complete.

28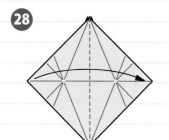

Repeat steps **25** – **27**
on the other side.

29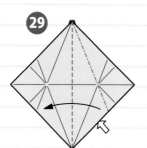

30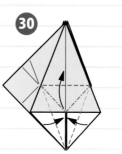

Petal fold (page 10).

31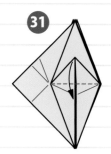

32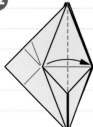

Swing over one flap.

33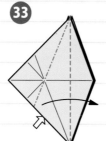

Repeat steps **29** – **32**
on the other side.

34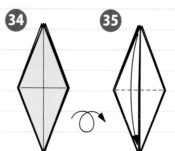

35

Fold the three other
sections in the same
way (**11** – **34**).

36

Swing over one flap.

End of the basic folds
Start applying glue on all the back sides of the tentacles

37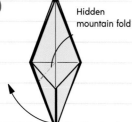

Hidden
mountain fold

Inside reverse fold
the top flap.

38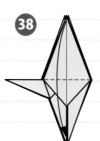

39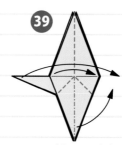

Fold over while
reverse folding.

40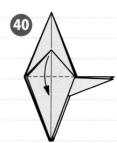

41

Fold over while reverse
folding. Allow the flaps
folded in steps **37** and
39 to swing behind.

42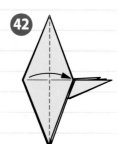

Fold the other flaps in the
same way (**36** – **41**), and
the overall shape should
become three-dimensional.

43

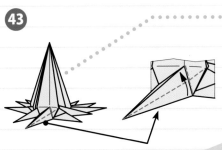

Valley fold each of the tentacles to make them thinner.

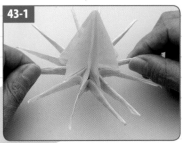

43-1

The structure after folding each of the tentacles.

43-2

The structure 43-1 from the back side. The eight corners in the middle will also become tentacles.

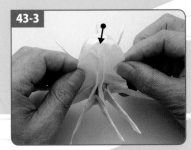

43-3

Squash fold the vertex.

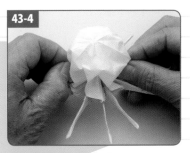

43-4

Squashing the vertex in progress.

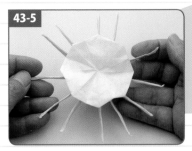

43-5

The structure from above after squashing the vertex.

43-6

Side view of 43-5.

43-7

Reverse fold the twelve tentacles so that they form right angles.

43-8

Add wrinkles to the top of the bell to add realism.

43-9

Thin the inner tentacles by folding.

43-10

Add cotton or tissue from the underside to achieve a full and solid shape.

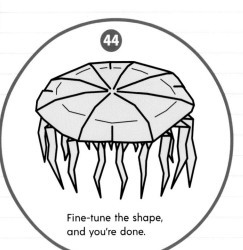

44

Fine-tune the shape, and you're done.

Published by Tuttle Publishing, an imprint of
Periplus Editions (HK) Ltd.

www.tuttlepublishing.com

REAL ORIGAMI MIZU NO NAKA WO OYOGU IKIMONO HEN
Copyright © 2016 Hisao Fukui
English translation rights arranged with KAWADE SHOBO
SHINSHA LTD. PUBLISHERS through Japan UNI Agency,
Inc., Tokyo

English Translation ©2020 Periplus Editions (HK) Ltd
Translated from Japanese by HL Language Services

ISBN 978-4-8053-1578-1

Staff (original Japanese edition)
Editing, text design and desktop publishing: Atelier Jam
(www.a-jam.com)
Editorial cooperation: Yamamoto Takatori
Photography: Maekawa Takehiko
Cover design: Sakamoto Hiroyuki / Atelier Jam

Distributed by
North America, Latin America & Europe
Tuttle Publishing
364 Innovation Drive
North Clarendon, VT 05759-9436 U.S.A.
Tel: (802) 773-8930 | Fax: (802) 773-6993
info@tuttlepublishing.com | www.tuttlepublishing.com

Japan
Tuttle Publishing
Yaekari Building, 3rd Floor
5-4-12 Osaki
Shinagawa-ku
Tokyo 141 0032
Tel: (81) 3 5437-0171 | Fax: (81) 3 5437-0755
sales@tuttle.co.jp | www.tuttle.co.jp

Asia Pacific
Berkeley Books Pte. Ltd.
3 Kallang Sector, #04-01
Singapore 349278
Tel: (65) 6741-2178 | Fax: (65) 6741-2179
inquiries@periplus.com.sg | www.tuttlepublishing.com

24 23 22 21 20   10 9 8 7 6 5 4 3 2 1
Printed in Malaysia   2009TO

Books to Span the East and West

Our core mission at Tuttle Publishing is to create books which bring people together one page at a time. Tuttle was founded in 1832 in the small New England town of Rutland, Vermont (USA). Our fundamental values remain as strong today as they were then—to publish best-in-class books informing the English-speaking world about the countries and peoples of Asia. The world is a smaller place today and Asia's economic, cultural and political influence has expanded, yet the need for meaningful dialogue and information about this diverse region has never been greater. Since 1948, Tuttle has been a leader in publishing books on the cultures, arts, cuisines, languages and literatures of Asia. Our authors and photographers have won many award and Tuttle has published thousands of titles on subjects ranging from martial arts to paper crafts. We welcome you to explore the wealth of information available on Asia at **www.tuttlepublishing.com**.

About the Author

Hisao Fukui was born in Shibuya Prefecture, Tokyo in 1951. He started creating origami models in 1971. His creations have been displayed at the Seibu Department store in the Shibuya, the PARCO store in Ikebukuro and other locations in Japan since 1974. He started focusing on new techniques to make more realistic three-dimensional origami some time around 1998. In 2002, he started holding monthly origami lessons at the Origami Center in Ochanomizu, Japan. In August, 2002, the Ochanomizu Origami Center held an origami exhibition of insects and dinosaurs, which would later be featured in the *Nihon Keizai* Newspaper. Hisao formed the Realistic Origami Association in September, 2002. In October, 2008, he received excellent reviews for his exhibition and work at Ebisu Garden Place. Hisao lives in Soka, Saitama where he also has an origami studio.

Ochanomizu Origami Center homepage:
www.origamikaikan.co.jp